ENGLISH MEN OF LETTERS

EDITED BY JOHN MORLEY

MATTHEW ARNOLD

MATTHEW ARNOLD

BY

HERBERT W. PAUL

New York

THE MACMILLAN COMPANY

LONDON: MACMILLAN & CO., Ltd.

1903

2768

Norwood Press
J. S. Cushing & Co. — Berwick & Smith Co.
Norwood, Mass., U.S.A.

PREFATORY NOTE

THE only authority for the events of Matthew Arnold's life, besides Mr. Richard Garnett's excellent article in the *Dictionary of National Biography*, is the collection of his letters in two volumes, edited by Mr. George Russell (Macmillan, 1895). Sir Joshua Fitch's account of Mr. Arnold's public services as Inspector of Schools in the seventh volume of *Great Educators* (Heinemann) is admirably clear, and Mr. Burnett Smart's *Bibliography* (The Dryden Press, 1892) cannot be overpraised. Professor Saintsbury's lively and learned study in Messrs. Blackwood's *Modern English Writers* (1899) is rather unsympathetic on the theological and political side, but full of interest and suggestion. I have sometimes owed most to Mr. Saintsbury when I have been least able to agree with him.

H. W. P.

CONTENTS

vii

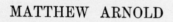
MATTHEW ARNOLD

MATTHEW ARNOLD

CHAPTER I

INTRODUCTORY

THE fourteen years which have elapsed since Matthew Arnold's death have added greatly to the number of his readers, especially the readers of his poems. No poet of modern times, perhaps no English poet of any time, appeals so directly and so exclusively to the cultivated taste of the educated classes. To say that a classical education was necessary for understanding him would perhaps be to go too far. But a capacity for appreciating form and style, the charm of rhythm and the beauty of words, is undoubtedly essential. It may be said of Mr. Arnold with truth, and it is his chief praise, that the more widely mental culture spreads, the higher his fame will be. He was not, indeed, a profound thinker. He did not illuminate, like Wordsworth, with a single flash, the abysses of man's nature, and the inmost recesses of the human soul. He was not, as Plato was, a spectator of all time and all existence. His aim was, as he said of Sophocles, to see life steadily, and see it whole. But he saw it as a scholar and a man of letters. He interpreted greater minds than his own. He almost fulfilled his ideal. He knew, so far at least as the

B   1

Western world is concerned, the best that had been said and thought in all ages. Next to Milton, he was the most learned of English poets.

How far Matthew Arnold will suffer from having been too much the child of his own age, it is as yet too soon to say. The "Zeit-Geist" has its limitations. It is the spirit of wisdom, not the spirit of a day, that is justified of all her children. "Thyrsis" is a very beautiful poem, not much less beautiful than "Adonais," though very unlike it. But Clough was not Keats. Keats is near to every one of us, while Clough is already far away. To Mr. Arnold, however, Clough was not merely a personal friend. He was the embodiment of Oxford in the thirties and forties, of a special type now rare, if not extinct. Matthew Arnold's passionate love of Oxford has inspired some of his noblest verse, and some of his most musical prose. All Oxford men know, or used to know, the exquisite sentences about the beautiful city with her dreaming towers, breathing the last enchantment of the middle age. It was the unreformed Oxford which Matthew Arnold knew, and he represented the high-water mark of what it could do. The "grand old fortifying classical curriculum" at which he laughed, and in which he believed, was seen at its best in the Oxford of those days. There was no "specialising." There were classics, and there were mathematics, and there was the river, and there was Headington Hill with Shotover beyond it. If that did not satisfy a man, he must have been hard to please. At any rate, he was not entitled to take a degree in Tamil, with a school and examiners all to himself.

Education was the business of Matthew Arnold's

life. He understood it in the broadest sense. There was nothing narrow, technical, or pedantic about his scholarship or his criticism. But in the proper sense of a much abused term his work is academic. It is steeped in, one might say saturated with, culture. It was written by a scholar for scholars, and only scholars can fully appreciate it. Matthew Arnold fulfilled the precept of Horace. He turned over his Greek models by day and by night. He brought everything to the classical touchstone. Whatever was not Greek was barbarian. "Except," wrote Sir Henry Maine, in a moment of rare enthusiasm, "except the blind forces of nature, nothing moves in this world which is not Greek in its origin." Such was substantially Mr. Arnold's creed, though as his father's son he recognised that Hebraism entered with Hellenism into the structure of the Christian Church.

Yet both as a poet and as a critic Matthew Arnold was essentially a man of his time. He was singularly receptive of ideas, even when they were ephemeral. He loved to dabble in politics, but the best parts of his political writings are the quotations from Burke. He did more than dabble in theology. He took the doctors of the Tübingen school for apostles, and treated a phase of Biblical speculation as if it were permanent truth. He had no sympathy with dry and minute criticism of detail, like Bishop Colenso's. He addicted himself to Ewald and to Renan. He threw himself into the Liberal reaction against Tractarianism, whose attitude to the Great First Cause has been described by a satirist in the memorable line —

" Philosophy is lenient ; he may go."

Matthew Arnold's literary criticism, once regarded by young enthusiasts as a revelation, has long since taken a secure place in English letters. Like his poetry, unlike his theology and his politics, it has original and intrinsic value. It is penetrating as well as brilliant, conscientious as well as imaginative. Matthew Arnold may be said to have done for literature almost what Ruskin did for art. He reminded, or informed, the British public that criticism was a serious thing; that good criticism was just as important as good authorship; that it was not a question of individual taste, but partly of received authority, and partly of trained judgment. His own masters, besides the old Greeks, were chiefly Goethe and Sainte-Beuve. But few critics have been so thoroughly original, and still fewer have had so large a share of the "dæmonic" faculty, the faculty which awakens intelligent enthusiasm in others. *Essays in Criticism* is one of the indispensable books. Not to have read it is to be ignorant of a great intellectual event.

In his double character of poet and critic, Matthew Arnold may be called our English Goethe. This is not to put the two men on a level; for, of course, one could not without absurdity talk of Goethe as a German Arnold. Goethe is one of the world's poets. Matthew Arnold is little known to those who do not speak the English tongue. But among them his reputation widens, and will widen, as knowledge and the love of books spread through all classes of society. To all who care for things of the mind his work must ever be dear. Something of his own radiant and sympathetic personality pervades all his writings, except perhaps when he is dealing with Dissenters. It would have been well if he had applied the critical pruning-knife to the exuberant mannerism which sometimes disfigures his style. The repetition of pet phrases is a literary vice. But Matthew Arnold is more than strong enough to live in spite of his faults. His best poetry, and his best prose, are among the choicest legacies bequeathed by the nineteenth century to the twentieth. If they belong to an age, they are the glory of it, for they show what golden ore it could extract, and hand down to the future, from the buried accumulations of the past.

CHAPTER II

Matthew Arnold was born at Laleham, near Staines, in the county of Middlesex, on Christmas Eve, 1822. Laleham is situated on the Thames, for which from his earliest years he had a passionate love. His father, Dr. Arnold of Rugby, the famous schoolmaster, had nine children, of whom Matthew was the eldest son. Mr. Thomas Arnold, however, did not become Dr. Arnold, or go to Rugby, till 1828. In 1822 he was taking private pupils, and forming the theories of education which he afterwards carried out in a more conspicuous field. His wife, born Mary Penrose, who lived till 1873, having survived her husband more than thirty years, was a woman of remarkable character and intellect, with whom Matthew kept up to the day of her death a mentally sympathetic as well as personally affectionate correspondence. When the family removed to Rugby, Matthew was five, but two years afterwards he returned to Laleham as the pupil of his uncle, the Reverend John Buckland. The country round Rugby is, as Dr. Arnold used pathetically to complain, among the dullest and ugliest in England. As a contrast he took a house at Fox How, near Grasmere, on the Rotha, where he spent most of the holidays with his wife and children. The eldest boy

6

thus grew up under the shadow of Wordsworth, whose brilliant and penetrating interpreter he was destined to become. In August 1836, being then thirteen and a half, Matthew was sent to Winchester, of which Dr. Moberly, an elegant scholar, long afterwards Bishop of Salisbury, had just been appointed headmaster. Dr. Arnold was himself a Wykehamist, and had a high opinion of his old school. But after a year, in August 1837, Matthew was removed from Winchester to be under his father's eye in the schoolhouse at Rugby, where he remained until he went up to Oxford in 1841.

Rugby under Arnold has been made familiar to millions of readers by *Tom Brown's School Days.* When Arnold was a candidate, Dr. Hawkins, the Provost of Oriel, prophesied that if elected he would revolutionise the public schools. He certainly revolutionised Rugby. When he came there, it was little more than an ordinary grammar school with boarders. When he died, it was one of the most famous and popular schools in England. The monitorial system was not really his invention. He introduced it from Winchester. But he invested it with a moral significance which had not previously belonged to it, and he leavened the whole school by his own powerful personality. As his accomplished biographer, Dean Stanley, says, "Throughout, whether in the school itself, or in its after effects, the one image that we have before us is not Rugby, but Arnold." Matthew Arnold bore very little resemblance to his stern Puritanical father. Dr. Arnold was in deadly earnest about everything, and was wholly devoid of humour. He was always declaiming against the childishness of boys, which after all is not a bad thing, and better than the premature mannishness which the monitorial system encourages. But he was in his way a great man. He had extraordinary force of character and strength of will. He had a magnetic influence upon boys. He was absolutely single-minded and sincere. His piety was deep and genuine, quite without suspicion of cant or conventionalism. His classical scholarship was not only sound and thorough, but broad, robust, and philosophical. As a teacher he stood high, as a preacher higher. There have been few better writers of English prose than Dr. Arnold, and it is perhaps his high literary sense which was his most distinctive bequest to his son. In a letter to his old pupil Vaughan, afterwards Master of the Temple, Dr. Arnold says: "There is an actual pleasure in contemplating so perfect a management of so perfect an instrument as is exhibited in Plato's language, even if the matter were as worthless as the words of Italian music; whereas the sense is only less admirable in many places than the language." But Thucydides was of course his favourite author; and the general reader, as distinguished from the philological student, can have at this day no better guide to the greatest of all historians than Dr. Arnold.

Dr. Arnold was, says Dean Stanley, "the elder brother and playfellow of his children." In that fine poem with the unfortunate metre, "Rugby Chapel," the son puts it rather differently: —

> " If, in the paths of the world,
>   Stones might have wounded thy feet,
>   Toil or dejection have tried
>   Thy spirit, of that we say

> Nothing ! To us thou wert still
> Cheerful, and helpful, and firm.
> Therefore to thee it was given
> Many to save with thyself ;
> And, at the end of thy day,
> O faithful shepherd ! to come,
> Bringing thy sheep in thy hand."

The thought expressed in these lines, the idea of a good man not content with saving his own soul, but devoting himself also to the salvation of others, is repeated in one of Matthew Arnold's most touching letters to his mother many years after his father's death. It was a singularly delightful trait in a most endearing character, that Mr. Arnold always in writing to her dwelt upon what "Papa" would have thought of things if he had been alive. Dr. Arnold died in 1842; and he was, thought his son, the first English clergyman who could speak as freely upon religious subjects as if he had been a layman. He was, however, strictly orthodox in all the essential doctrines of the Christian faith. He was suspected of heresy on no better grounds than his dislike of the Oxford Movement, which was strong, and his knowledge of German, which was thorough. He took the Liberal side in the first Hampden controversy, but the charges against Dr. Hampden completely broke down. In politics he was a decided, though independent Whig, and he wrote a pamphlet in favour of Catholic Emancipation. Yet he held as firmly as Mr. Gladstone once held the theory of a Christian state, and he consistently opposed the enfranchisement of the Jews. In one respect he was far in advance of his age. "Woe," he said, "to the generation which inhab-

its England when the coal-fields are exhausted, and the
National Debt has not been paid." Although he died
four years before the Repeal of the Corn Laws, he was
a staunch advocate of free exchange. It is impossible
not to trace the influence of the father in the politics
of the son.

We have the authority of Matthew Arnold's oldest
and most intimate friend, Lord Coleridge, for the fact,
which might perhaps have been surmised, that between
father and son there was more affection than sympathy.
Dr. Arnold abhorred "mere cleverness," and humour
appeared to him a rather profane indiscretion. His
eldest son was excessively clever, and full of a gaiety
which he never at any time of life made the smallest
attempt to subdue. Lord Coleridge hints that there
were collisions between them, and one can partly
believe it. But he adds that when the doctor had
trouble, as even schoolmasters sometimes have, he
found comfort in the filial piety of one whose genius
he did not live to acknowledge. The only poem of
Matthew Arnold's which his father saw was "Alaric
at Rome," recited in Rugby School on the 12th of June
1840. The motto from *Childe Harold*, prefixed to this
composition, prepares one for its character, which is
distinctly Byronic. It is not much above the ordinary
level of such things, and many men have written as
good verses when they were boys, who never came
within measurable distance of being poets. One
stanza, however, deserves to be quoted, because the
first two lines are the earliest example of a figure the
writer often afterwards employed : —

   " Yes, there are stories registered on high,
     Yes, there are stains time's fingers cannot blot,

> Deeds that shall live when they who did them, die ;
> Things that may cease, but never be forgot :
> Yet some there are, their very lives would give
> To be remember'd thus, and yet they cannot live."

The last couplet is sadly wooden, and shows that the young versifier had not got his stride. Macaulay is almost the only man who has successfully imitated without parodying Byron.

In this same year, 1840, Matthew Arnold won an open scholarship at Balliol, and in 1841 he went into residence. Oxford was then in the full swing of the Tractarian movement. Newman had not yet retired to Littlemore, and was still drawing crowded congregations at St. Mary's. The fascination of that extraordinary man attracted minds so utterly dissimilar to his own as Mark Pattison's and Anthony Froude's. But upon Matthew Arnold he seems to have had no effect whatever. Perhaps the influence of Dr. Arnold, who regarded Newman as something very like Antichrist, was too strong. In 1841, just before the Whigs went out of office, Lord Melbourne appointed Dr. Arnold Regius Professor of History, and in December of that year, to a crowded audience, largely composed of old Rugbeians, he delivered his inaugural lecture. In the following June he died, and his memory was consecrated by his early death. Matthew Arnold's own temperament, however, though not irreligious, was utterly unclerical, and he never contemplated, as most undergraduates not in easy circumstances at that time did, the possibility of taking orders.

Except for a few venerable landmarks, and the examination in the school of *Literæ Humaniores*, there

is little left now of the Oxford which Matthew Arnold
entered sixty years ago. Before the Commission of
1850 the University was in form what it had been in
the middle ages. All power was in the hands of the
Hebdomadal Board, and the Hebdomadal Board was
simply the Heads of Houses. The separate Colleges
kept strictly to themselves, there were no combined
lectures, and no unattached students. Every undergraduate subscribed the Thirty-Nine Articles, so that
only members of the Church of England could enter
the University.

Such, at least, was the theory, though of course in
practice religious tests exclude only the conscientious.
But a society confined to one ecclesiastical organisation
gave itself up to the vehemence of ecclesiastical disputes. Nonconformity was not represented. Rome
proved a powerful attraction, and young men, as Pattison puts it, spent the time that should have been
devoted to study in discussing which was the true
Church. At Balliol there was perhaps more intellectual activity than at any other college. The scholarships and fellowships, as was rare in those days, were
open. Dr. Jenkyns, the Master, though no great
scholar himself, was jealous for Balliol's intellectual
reputation, and had some at least of the qualities
which in a larger world are called statesmanship.
Mr. Jowett, then a young Fellow, was beginning the
long career which will always be associated with the
name of Balliol. Of Dr. Arnold's old pupils at Balliol,
Stanley had become a Fellow of University, and
Clough a Fellow of Oriel. Among Matthew Arnold's
contemporaries his closest friends were John Duke
Coleridge, afterwards Lord Chief-Justice of England,

and John Campbell Shairp, afterwards Principal of the
United College, St. Andrew's.   Shairp's lines about
Matthew Arnold are too hackneyed for quotation.
They describe the debonair gaiety with which all his
friends are familiar, and which he never lost.   The
" home of lost causes, and forsaken beliefs, and unpopular names, and impossible loyalties," was dearer to Mr.
Arnold than Rugby, or even Laleham.   For the country
round Oxford he had a passion, which found full vent
in "The Scholar Gipsy" and in "Thyrsis."   For the
squabbles about Tract Number Ninety, and " Ideal
Ward's " Degree, he did not care two straws.   Max
Müller has described in his Autobiography the amaze-
ment which he, a young German, fresh from Leipzig
and Berlin, felt at the spectacle of religious disputes
having no intelligible connection with religion.   Matthew Arnold's view of them was much the same as
Max Müller's.

In the year after his father's death, 1843, Matthew
Arnold won the Newdigate with a poem on "Cromwell."
He and Tennyson are exceptions to the rule that prizes
for poetry do not fall to poets.   But " Cromwell " is
even less remarkable than " Alaric at Rome."   Written,
as all Newdigates must be, in heroic rhyme, it has flow
and smoothness of numbers without inspiration, or
even distinction of style.   There is one obvious touch
of Wordsworth, or, as some will have it, of Wordsworth's wife —

> " Yet all high sounds that mountain children hear
>   Flash'd from thy soul upon thine inward ear."

But Wordsworth had as yet no reason to be proud of
his pupil.   There is more promise of the future in the

Rugby poem than in the Oxford one, and more of the
feeling for nature which was afterwards so conspicuous.
Matthew Arnold's published Letters unfortunately do
not date back to his Oxford days, which must have
been among the fullest and the most enjoyable of his
full and happy life.   We know from Lord Coleridge
that he belonged to " The Decade," a small debating
Society, where, as that great lover of argument says,
they " fought to the stumps of their intellects."   Perhaps the poet neglected the schools.   At any rate, like
his friend Clough a few years before him, he was placed
in the second class at the final examination for Classical
Honours.   But this comparative failure was more than
redeemed, in his case as in Clough's, by a Fellowship at
Oriel, of which his father had also been a Fellow.   He
was elected in 1845, when an Oriel Fellowship was still
regarded as the most brilliant crown of an Oxford
career.   Dr. Hawkins, the famous Provost, who brought
to the government of a college an ability greater than
has often been employed in the misgovernment of
kingdoms, would not allow a vacancy to be advertised.
If people, he said, wanted to know whether there was
a vacant Fellowship at Oriel, they might come and
ask.   Certainly the College of Whately and Newman,
of Clough and Church, of Matthew Arnold and his
father, had good reason to be proud of its sons.   But
it would not have suited Matthew Arnold to become a
College Don.   He was essentially a man of the world,
loving society in its widest sense, a scholar by temperament and taste, but delighting to mix with all sorts
and conditions of his fellow-creatures.   Although, like
most Oxford men of his generation, he had no scientific
bent or training, his interests were too many rather

than too few. Narrowness was never among his faults. He was rather too apt to think that there was no subject upon which an educated man is not competent to form an opinion. Perhaps the free life of unreformed Oxford, with its lax discipline, its few examinations, its ample leisure for social intercourse of the best and highest kind, as of others with which the biographer of Matthew Arnold has no concern, fostered a tendency to diffusiveness, as well as a belief that everything was open for discussion. As a critic Matthew Arnold was not free from a dogmatism of his own. But the chief lesson which he took away from Oxford was the Platonic maxim, βίος ἀνεξέταστος οὐ βιωτός, — "life without the spirit of inquiry is not worth living."

CHAPTER III

EARLY POEMS

AFTER taking his degree, which would have shocked his father, and winning his Fellowship, which would have delighted him, Matthew Arnold returned to Rugby, and taught classics in the fifth form. Thus began his long connection with education, which only ceased two years before his death. Dr. Arnold's successor in the headmastership of Rugby was Dr. Tait, a less brilliant scholar, but a man of great dignity and profound sagacity, whose full powers were not tested until he came to direct the Church of England, and to represent her in the House of Lords, at a period of momentous interest and importance. It is not too much to say that no other public school in England has been governed within so short a time by three men so able, eminent, and influential as Dr. Arnold, Dr. Tait, and Dr. Temple. Two of them became Archbishops of Canterbury. The third might have eclipsed them both if he had not been cut off prematurely in the plenitude of his physical and intellectual vigour. It is curious that not one of them was a Rugby man. Many years afterwards, at a dinner given within the walls of Balliol, Mr. Arnold, with characteristic irony and urbanity, contrasted Archbishop Tait and himself as types of the Balliol man who had succeeded and the

Balliol man who had failed in life.   It is probable that
these few months at Rugby improved and confirmed
the accuracy of Matthew Arnold's scholarship, which
distinguishes his classical poems, and his "Lectures on
Translating Homer."   There is a good deal more to be
said for gerund-grinding than Carlyle would allow.

Mr. Arnold, however, was not destined to remain
long a schoolmaster.   He soon became the citizen of a
larger world than Rugby, and few indeed have been
better qualified to instruct or to adorn it.   In 1847 he
was made private secretary to Lord Lansdowne, then
President of the Council in the administration of Lord
John Russell.   Lord Lansdowne was one of those
statesmen who play a great part in political history
without filling a large space in the newspapers.
Without striking abilities, and without ambition of
any kind, he contrived by his personal tact and calm
wisdom to reconcile the differences of the Whig party,
to keep more brilliant men than himself out of mischief, and to lead the House of Lords.   He had also
the pleasant and valuable gift of recognising early
promise, together with the rare and enviable power
of bringing young men forward and giving them their
chance.   It was he who brought Macaulay into the
House of Commons as Member for Calne, and to him
the country owes it that Matthew Arnold had the
opportunity of doing for popular education what no
one else could have done.   He was a real, though a
very moderate, Liberal, and Matthew Arnold's politics
were substantially those of his patron.

The earliest of Mr. Arnold's Letters, edited by
Mr. George Russell, and published by Messrs. Macmillan, is dated the 2nd of January 1848, on his way to

c

Bowood, Lord Lansdowne's house in Wiltshire. It was apparently his first visit, for he tells his mother, to whom the letter is written, that he does not expect to "know a soul there." But Matthew Arnold was never shy ; and Lord Lansdowne, as Macaulay testifies, was the most gracious of hosts. Of the society of Bowood, however, we have in the letters no glimpse. On this January day in the year of Revolutions the writer had come from his old home at Laleham, and he gives an enthusiastic description of the country. " Yesterday," he says, "I was at Chertsey, the poetic town of our childhood, as opposed to the practical, historical Staines; it is *across* the river, reached by no bridges and roads, but by the primitive ferry, the meadow path, the Abbey river with its wooden bridge, and the narrow lane by the old wall; and, itself the stillest of country towns backed by St. Ann's, leads nowhere but to the heaths and pines of Surrey. How unlike the journey to Staines, and the great road through the flat, drained Middlesex plain, with its single standing pollarded elms." No English poet, not even Wordsworth, had a more passionate love of the country than Matthew Arnold. But, unlike Wordsworth, he was an omnivorous reader, as familiar with German and French as with Latin and Greek. Writing again to his mother on the 7th of May in this same year 1848, he expresses a rather crude and hasty verdict on Heine, to whom he afterwards did more justice both in prose and verse. "I have just finished," he tells Mrs. Arnold, "a German book I brought with me here, a mixture of poems and travelling journal by Heinrich Heine, the most famous of the young German literary set. He has a good deal of power, though more trick ;

however, he has thoroughly disgusted me. The
Byronism of a German, of a man trying to be gloomy,
cynical, impassioned, *moqueur*, etc., all *à la fois*, with
their honest bonhommistic language and total want of
experience of the kind that Lord Byron, an English
peer with access everywhere, possessed, is the most
ridiculous thing in the world." Happily, Matthew
Arnold travelled soon and far from the state of mind
in which he could regard the *Reisebilder* as "the most
ridiculous thing in the world." The author of *Heine's
Grave* knew that to speak of Heine as a man who
tried to be gloomy was the reverse of the truth.
Heine's model was not Byron, but Sterne, and it was
beneath Matthew Arnold to bring the privileges of
the peerage into literature. But there never was a
more flagrant example than Byron in contradiction of
the proverb *Noblesse oblige*, and it cannot be denied
that Dr. Arnold would have highly disapproved of the
Reisebilder.

On the 21st of July 1849 there appeared in the
Examiner the first of Matthew Arnold's sonnets. It
was published anonymously, and addressed "To the
Hungarian Nation." On the 29th of July he told his
mother that it was "not worth much," and from this
candid opinion I, at least, am not prepared to dissent.
Such lines as

> " Not in American vulgarity,
>   Nor wordy German imbecility,"

would almost have justified a repetition of the prophecy which Dryden delivered to Swift. And yet, before the year was over, Mr. Arnold had brought out a
volume which ought to have established his place in

English poetry, though for some unexplained reason it did not. The "Sonnet to the Hungarian Nation" was not republished in the lifetime of the author. It may be found in *Alaric at Rome and Other Poems,* edited by Mr. Richard Garnett in 1896.

The Strayed Reveller and Other Poems, by "A.," appeared in the author's twenty-seventh year. Few volumes of equal merit have made so small an impression upon the public. Although every poem in it, except one, "The Hayswater Boat," was afterwards reprinted with Mr. Arnold's sanction, and now forms a permanent part of English literature, scarcely any notice was taken of it at the time, and it was withdrawn from circulation when only a few copies had been sold. It is difficult to account for this neglect. The age was not altogether a prosaic one. Wordsworth was still alive, and still Laureate, although it was long since he had written anything that wore the semblance of inspiration. Tennyson was already famous, in spite of envious detraction and ignorant misunderstanding. Browning, though not yet popular, was ardently admired as the author of "Paracelsus" by a small circle of the best judges. Rogers was enjoying in his old age a poetical reputation which, though it may have been enhanced by his social celebrity, was yet thoroughly deserved. Matthew Arnold, unlike them all, was as true a poet as any of them, and had none of the obscurity which made Browning "caviare to the general." So far as the poem which gave its title to the book is concerned, the cold reception accorded to it was natural enough. Rhyme and blank verse have their own high and recognised positions. We may agree with Milton in

holding that rhyme is "no necessary adjunct" of
"poem or good verse," while yet humbly and rever-
ently dissenting from his further opinion that it was
"the invention of a barbarous age to set off wretched
matter and lame metre," which indeed the noble and
beautiful melody of "Lycidas" and "Comus" and
"L'Allegro" and "Il Penseroso" sufficiently refutes.
But except for a few hexameters, such as some of
Kingsley's, some of Longfellow's, all Dr. Hawtrey's,
and a few of Clough's, there is hardly room in English
for verse which is neither one nor the other. I say
"hardly," remembering Tennyson's "Gleam" and
Browning's "One Word More." But I do not think
that any poem of Matthew Arnold's, not even "Rugby
Chapel," could be included in the same category as
these. *The Strayed Reveller* opens well with the
impassioned address of the youth to Circe —

> "Faster, faster,
>   O Circe, Goddess,
> Let the wild, thronging train,
>   The bright procession
>   Of eddying forms,
>   Sweep through my soul."

But a line which almost immediately follows —

> "Leān'd ŭp ăgainst thĕ cŏlūmn there,"

is surely cacophonous to the last degree. The idea
of the poem is as fascinating as it is fantastic. The
spells of Circe have wrought no hideous transforma-
tion here. The youth's visions are the visions of the
gods, and the appearance of Ulysses, the "spare, dark-
featur'd, quick-eyed stranger," recalls that wonderful
line, which sums up the spirit of all adventure —

> "πλεῖν ἐπὶ οἴνοπα πόντον, ἐπ' ἀλλοθρόους ἀνθρώπους."

But poets, from the least to the greatest, have to reckon with the necessity of external form.

The "Fragment of an 'Antigone'" is a similar experiment, and not in my opinion more successful. Such lines as

> "August laws doth mightily vindicate,"

or

> "A dead, ignorant, thankless corpse,"

require an abnormal ear to appreciate their harmony. Moreover, this piece suffers by comparison with Mr. Browning's stately fragment of an Hippolytus called "Artemis Prologises," and with Cardinal Newman's verses, beginning "Man is permitted many things." They have beauty of form, and are cast in national moulds, for one is blank verse, and the other is rhyme.

But these are spots on the sun. The little book, so soon suppressed, contained some of Mr. Arnold's best work, and should have received, at least from all scholars, an enthusiastic welcome. The opening sonnet, suggested by Goethe's famous "Ohne Hast ohne Rast," is not equal to the later ones on Homer, Epictetus, and Sophocles, which may perhaps be called his best. But it raises at once the question where Matthew Arnold's sonnets deserve to rank. No one, I suppose, would class them with Keats's or with Wordsworth's. They might fairly be put on a level with Rossetti's, and above Tennyson's, for Tennyson did not shine in the very difficult art of sonnet-writing. It may be considered a proof rather of Mr. Arnold's courage than of his discretion that he should have written a sonnet on Shakespeare. Shakespeare's own sonnets are beacons, and, like other beacons, they

are warnings.   Of fine writing on Shakespeare we
have enough, and more than enough.

"Self-school'd, self-scann'd, self-honour'd, self-secure,"

is but fine writing after all.   The sonnet "Written in
Emerson's Essays" is thoughtful and interesting.   But
the last line is open to an obvious criticism —

"Dumb judges, answer, truth or mockery?"

What is the use of asking dumb judges to answer?
The lines "To an Independent Preacher, who preached
that we should be in Harmony with Nature," lack the
urbanity which Mr. Arnold always preached, and usually practised.   But contact with Dissenters seems to
have upset his moral equilibrium.   The finest of these
early sonnets is the first of the three addressed "To
a Republican Friend."   The friend was, I presume,
Clough, to whom he wrote as "Citizen Clough, Oriel
Lyceum, Oxford," assuring him, as Clough tells us,
that "the Millennium was not coming this bout."
Clough's republicanism was skin-deep, and before his
premature death he might have said, with Southey,
that he was no more ashamed of having been a republican than of having been young.   Many Oxford
Liberals, Stanley included, were enthusiastic demo-
crats in 1849, when France seemed to be showing the
way, and no one suspected that the Second Empire
was at hand.   But few, indeed, except John Duke
Coleridge, retained their early faith to the end of
their days.   Matthew Arnold, however, was from the
first a moderate Liberal, and a moderate Liberal he
continued to the last.   The excellent qualities of
judgment and sympathy were his, but of political

enthusiasm he was incapable. This beautiful sonnet
deserves to be quoted at length, not only for its
intrinsic merits, but also because it is thoroughly
characteristic of his thoughts and wishes —

> " God knows it, I am with you. If to prize
> Those virtues, priz'd and practis'd by too few,
> But priz'd, but lov'd, but eminent in you,
> Man's fundamental life : if to despise
> The barren optimistic sophistries
> Of comfortable moles, whom what they do
> Teaches the limit of the just and true —
> And for such doing have no need of eyes :
> If sadness at the long heart-wasting show
> Wherein earth's great ones are disquieted :
> If thoughts, not idle, while before me flow
> The armies of the homeless and unfed : —
> If these are yours, if this is what you are,
> Then am I yours, and what you feel, I share."

This is not equal to Wordsworth's incomparable
sonnet on Milton, which it inevitably suggests, but
they are very noble lines, and they contain the essence
of Mr. Arnold's political creed.

Readers must have been blind, indeed, who could
not see the beauty of "Mycerinus." The strange,
weird, tragic story of this Egyptian king is familiar
to all lovers of Herodotus. In that exquisitely simple
and pellucid style which none of his successors have
equalled or approached the unconsciously great historian tells how Mycerinus forsook the evil ways of
his cruel father, and governed his people with a mild,
paternal rule. The father lived to a green old age,
feared and hated by his subjects. Against the son in
the prime of life there went out a decree from the

oracles of God that after six years he must die. Vainly did Mycerinus protest that, shunning bad examples, he had loved justice and hated iniquity. The stern answer came that he had misread the sentence of fate, which had determined that for a century the Egyptians should be oppressed. The father was wiser in his generation than the child of light. Then Mycerinus felt that the riddle of the painful earth was more than he could read; that to struggle was useless; and that all he could do was to make his six years into twelve by devoting every moment to pleasure, by turning night into day. But first he summoned the people, and told them the whole story. He described briefly his own youth —

> " Self-govern'd, at the feet of Law;
> Ennobling this dull pomp, the life of kings,
> By contemplation of diviner things."

He took them into his confidence. He asked them, as if they could tell him, whether the gods were altogether careless of men and men's actions.

> " Or is it that some Power, too wise, too strong,
> Even for yourselves to conquer or beguile,
> Whirls earth, and heaven, and men, and gods along,
> Like the broad rushing of the column'd Nile?
> And the great powers we serve, themselves may be
> Slaves of a tyrannous Necessity ? "

No such verse had been written in English since Wordsworth's "Laodamia," and the poem abounds in single lines of haunting charm, such as —

> " Love, free to range, and regal banquetings,"

> " Sweep in the sounding stillness of the night,"

which has an echo of Theocritus, with perfect couplets, as, for instance —

> " And prayers, and gifts, and tears, are fruitless all,
>   And the night waxes, and the shadows fall."

Or, in the concluding portion of the poem, which is blank verse —

> " While the deep-burnish'd foliage overhead
>   Splinter'd the silver arrows of the moon,"

where the Virgilian note will strike every scholar. "Stand forth, true poet that you are," should have been the discerning critic's invitation to the anonymous author of " Mycerinus." But it was not.

The contents of this little volume varied much in merit, as in other respects. " The Sick King in Bokhara " is almost prosaic. Mr. Arnold, who hated Macaulay, sneered at the *Lays of Ancient Rome*, of which his father was so fond, and selected for especial ridicule the lines from " Horatius " —

> " To every man upon this earth
>   Death cometh, soon or late."

There is not much to be said for them, I admit. But if a poet is to be judged by his worst things, and not by his best, there are lines from " The Sick King in Bokhara " which may be set beside Macaulay's —

> " Look, this is but one single place,
>   Though it be great : all the earth round,
>   If a man bear to have it so,
>   Things which might vex him shall be found."

If this is poetry, what is prose ? Although I may be rash, I give my opinion for what it is worth, and it is that neither the story of this invalid monarch nor

Mr. Arnold's treatment of it made the poem meet for republication, or for anything but repentance.

"A Modern Sappho," in the style of Moore's *Irish Melodies*, is chiefly memorable for the fine couplet —

> " But deeper their voice grows, and nobler their bearing,
>   Whose youth in the fires of anguish hath died."

"The New Sirens" is an especial favourite with Mr. Swinburne, and was republished a quarter of a century afterwards at his request. No poet has been more generously appreciative of his contemporaries, whether older or younger than himself, than Mr. Swinburne; and in this case, at all events, his insight was sure. "The New Sirens" is not unlike Mrs. Browning's "Wine of Cyprus," but it is less unequal, more musical, more chastened and subdued. The poem "To a Gipsy Child by the Seashore" contains one most beautiful quatrain —

> " Ah ! not the nectarous poppy lovers use,
>   Not daily labour's dull, Lethæan spring,
>   Oblivion in lost angels can infuse
>   Of the soil'd glory, and the trailing wing."

A critic of the Johnsonian school, however, might observe that it is the unsoiled glory and the soaring wing which the lost angels would remember. Remembrance is of the past, not the present. In its delicate loveliness "The Forsaken Merman" ranks high among Mr. Arnold's poems. It is a story of a Sea-king, married to a mortal maiden, who forsook him and her children under the impulse of a Christian conviction that she must return and pray for her soul. Her name was Mr. Arnold's favourite name, Margaret.

The Merman saw her through the window as she sat
in church with her eyes on "the holy book." But she
came back to him no more. "Alone dwell for ever
the kings of the sea." "Alone the sun rises, and alone
Spring the great streams," says Mr. Arnold in another
poem.

Perhaps the most exquisite, and certainly the most
characteristic, poem in the volume is "Resignation."
One cannot doubt that into these lines of chiselled
and classic perfection Matthew Arnold put his mind
and soul. Everything in the book was republished,
except "The Hayswater Boat," which hardly deserved
exclusion. But "Resignation" is part of Mr. Arnold's
life and character. We cannot think of him without
it. At the very beginning we read of "the Goth, bound
Rome-wards," and we remember Alaric. The "mist-
wreath'd flock" and the "wet flower'd grass" recall
the Sicilian poet he loved so well. But Theocritus is
not the poet described here —

> "Lean'd on his gate, he gazes : tears
> Are in his eyes, and in his ears
> The murmur of a thousand years ;
> Before him he sees Life unroll,
> A placid and continuous whole ;
> That general Life, which does not cease,
> Whose secret is not joy, but peace ;
> That Life, whose dumb wish is not miss'd
> If birth proceeds, if things subsist ;
> The Life of plants, and stones, and rain ;
> The Life he craves ; if not in vain
> Fate gave, what Chance shall not control,
> His sad lucidity of soul."

If Mr. Arnold was, as he must have been, sometimes
sad, he never allowed the shadow of his gloom to rest

upon others. Peace of mind and lucidity of soul he
acquired, if he did not always possess them. Probably they were congenital, like the healthier and
sounder parts of his father's Puritanism. A fastidious
critic, Tennyson for instance, might have objected to
the juxtaposition of " gate " and " gazes," or of " wish "
and " miss'd." But apart from small blemishes of this
kind, the lines are as symmetrical in form as they
are full of calm and yet intense feeling. They sum
up Mr. Arnold's imaginative philosophy. They are
the man. Equal to them, perhaps in expression beyond
them, are those which almost immediately follow: —

> " Deeply the Poet feels ; but he
>   Breathes, when he will, immortal air,
>   Where Orpheus and where Homer are.
>   In the day's life, whose iron round
>   Hems us all in, he is not bound.
>   He escapes thence, but we abide.
>   Not deep the Poet sees, but wide."

Shakespeare was not the only poet who saw deep as
well as wide. It would be hard to fathom the thought
of Wordsworth in his sublimest moments, and Orpheus
was a mystic, if Homer was not. Sophocles was
perhaps in Mr. Arnold's mind — " singer of sweet
Colonos, and its child." He never surpassed the best
things in " Resignation," and for life's fitful fever the
English language, rich as it is in all manner of refreshing influences, contains no more healing balm.

CHAPTER IV

On the 14th of April 1851, Matthew Arnold was appointed by Lord Lansdowne to an Inspectorship of Schools, which he retained for five-and-thirty years. His friend, Mr. Ralph Lingen, afterwards Lord Lingen, who had been his tutor at Oxford, was influential in procuring him this post, though it came to him naturally enough, being in the gift of his official chief. Mr. Lingen was Secretary to the Education Department, then in its infancy, and he wished to attract young men of promise from the Universities. He never made a better choice than Matthew Arnold. It is no disparagement of the many able men who have been Inspectors of Schools to say that not one of them excelled Mr. Arnold in fitness for the post. He was very fond of children, he knew by instinct how to deal with them, and at the other end of the scale he had a real scientific knowledge of what education in its highest sense ought to be. With lofty ideas of that kind, however, he had for some years little enough to do. Compulsory education was still the dream of advanced theorists. The parliamentary grants were only five years old, and a school which chose, like Archdeacon Denison's, to dispense with a grant, could dispense with inspection too. But the bribe was pretty high, few national schools could afford to despise it, and Mr. Arnold had plenty to do. Throughout his life, indeed, he worked hard for a moderate salary, never complaining, always promoting the happiness of others, and throwing into his daily duties every power of his mind. In one of his early letters to his sister, Mrs. Forster, Mr. Arnold naïvely observes that he is much more worldly than the rest of his family. He was fond of society, and a delightful member of it. Worldly in any other sense he was not. Few men have had less ambition, or a stronger sense of duty. On the 10th of June, in this same year, he married the lady who for the rest of his life was the chief source of his happiness. Her name was Frances Lucy Wightman, and her father was an excellent Judge of a good old school, much respected in Court, little known outside. Mr. Arnold, though neither a lawyer nor interested in law, accompanied Mr. Justice Wightman on circuit for many Assizes as Marshal. Characteristically avoiding the criminal side, he liked to watch his father-in-law try causes. " He does it so admirably," he tells his wife. " It " is said to be a lost art.

One of his first letters to Mrs. Arnold, dated from the Oldham Road Lancastrian School at Manchester, on the 15th of October 1851, shows the spirit with which he entered upon his regular functions. " I think I shall get interested in the schools after a little time," he writes ; "their effects on the children are so immense, and their future effects in civilising the next generation of the lower classes, who, as things are going, will have most of the political power of the country in their hands, may be so important." But meanwhile he gave the public another volume of poems.

In October 1852 appeared *Empedocles on Etna, and Other Poems*, by "A." Although this volume, with its predecessor, contains most of Mr. Arnold's best verse, and although he never afterwards wrote anything except "Thyrsis" and "Westminster Abbey," which added much to his poetical reputation, the one book fell as flat as the other, and was withdrawn before fifty copies had been sold. A greater reproach to the criticism of the early Victorian age there could hardly be. Tennyson had succeeded Wordsworth as Poet Laureate, but he had not yet become really popular, and Browning was still only the idol of a clique. The one man in England fit to be compared with either Browning or Tennyson gave the public of his best, and the public neither praised nor blamed. They took no notice at all. The earliest of these most varied and interesting poems in point of time is the "Memorial Verses" on the death of Wordsworth, which happened in April 1850. The opening lines are familiar —

> " Goethe in Weimar sleeps, and Greece,
> Long since, saw Byron's struggle cease.
> But one such death remain'd to come.
> The last poetic verse is dumb.
> What shall be said o'er Wordsworth's tomb ? "

To Tennyson, Matthew Arnold was always unjust, and never appreciated his greatness. Whether "tomb" rhymes with "dumb" I shall not assume the province of determining. Mr. Arnold had not a faultless ear. Indeed, some of his unrhymed lyrics lead one to ask whether he had any ear at all, and for richness of melody he cannot be mentioned with Mr. Swinburne. Goethe and Wordsworth can hardly be compared,

except for purposes of contrast. Wordsworth, as is
well known, objected to Goethe's poetry that it was
"not inevitable enough," thereby introducing a word
which has since been done to death in the service of
the lower criticism. But Mr. Arnold's classic eulogy
of Goethe is fine in itself, being indeed little more than
a paraphrase of the great Virgilian hexameters —

> " Felix qui potuit rerum cognoscere causas,
>   Atque metus omnes, et inexorabile fatum,
>   Subjecit pedibus, strepitumque Acherontis Averni."

When we read —

> " Time may restore us in his course
>   Goethe's sage mind and Byron's force ;
>   But where will Europe's latter hour
>   Again find Wordsworth's healing power ? "

we are tempted to ask why another Wordsworth is
less possible, if there can be degrees of possibility,
than another Goethe ? And indeed much of the healing power may be found in the best verse of Mr.
Arnold himself.

Empedocles on Etna was a special favourite with
Robert Browning, at whose request it reappeared in
1867. It was then new as a whole to the general
public, for in 1852 its author almost immediately withdrew it, and only fragments of it were reprinted in
1855. That Browning should admire it was not
wonderful, for both the subject and the treatment are
suggestive of " Paracelsus," though " Paracelsus " is to
my thinking a far finer poem. Empedocles was a
Sicilian Greek of the fifth century before Christ, whose
philosophical remains, such as they are, show him to
have been a dreamy, mystical sceptic. The legend

D

that in despair of attaining truth, he flung himself into the crater of Etna, is a mere tradition without historic value. The blank verse of Empedocles is not equal to Mr. Arnold's best. Such a line as —

" I hear, Gorgias, their chief, speaks nobly of him,"

can neither be defended nor scanned. On the other hand —

" The Adriatic breaks in a warm bay,"

is a masterpiece of its kind. The unrhymed lyrics are, to speak plainly, both here and throughout this volume, detestable —

" Great qualities are trodden down,
   And littleness united
   Is become invincible."

This is not poetry. It is scarcely even prose. It is something for which literature has no name. The song of Empedocles to his harp, though far below "Rabbi Ben Ezra," contains some striking verses, as, for instance —

" We would have inward peace,
   Yet will not look within :
   We would have misery cease,
   Yet will not cease from sin,"

where the curiously Christian tone of Greek moral philosophy is well brought out. But the best parts of the drama, if drama it is to be called, are the songs of Callicles. There is one passage clearly written under the influence of Gray, with whom Mr. Arnold has sometimes, not perhaps to much purpose, been compared —

" And the Eagle, at the beck
   Of the appeasing gracious harmony,

> Droops all his sheeny, brown, deep-feather'd neck,
> Nestling nearer to Jove's feet :
> While o'er his sovereign eye
> The curtains of the blue films slowly meet."

One instinctively recalls the beautiful couplet in the
" Progress of Poesy "—

> " Quenched in dark clouds of slumber lie
> The terrors of his beak, and lightnings of his eye."

The best consecutive passage of blank verse in the
poem is undoubtedly the following —

> " And yet what days were those, Parmenides !
> When we were young, when we could number friends
> In all the Italian cities like ourselves,
> When with elated hearts we join'd your train,
> Ye Sun-born virgins ! on the road of Truth.
> Then we could still enjoy, then neither thought
> Nor outward things were clos'd and dead to us,
> But we received the shock of mighty thoughts
> On simple minds with a pure natural joy,
> And if the sacred load oppress'd our brain,
> We had the power to feel the pressure eas'd,
> The brow unbound, the thought flow free again,
> In the delightful commerce of the world."

This is truly Wordsworthian, though Wordsworth
would hardly have ended two lines out of three with
the same substantive. But the song of Callicles at
the end is the gem of the piece. The stanzas are
familiar —

> " Not here, O Apollo !
> Are haunts meet for thee.
> But, where Helicon breaks down
> In cliff to the sea."

Here the third line halts badly. This, however, is
almost perfect —

> " 'Tis Apollo comes leading
> His choir, The Nine.
> — The Leader is fairest,
> But all are divine."

These, too, are lovely, though perhaps the word
"hotness" is exceptionable —

> " First hymn they the Father
> Of all things : and then
> The rest of Immortals,
> The action of men.
>
> The Day in its hotness,
> The strife with the palm ;
> The Night in its silence,
> The Stars in their calm."

The question why the second of these two stanzas is
inferior to the first lies at the root of poetry, and
involves the true value of poetic style.

The other long poem in this volume, "Tristram and
Iseult," contains some of Mr. Arnold's best lyrics,
especially the noble stanza beginning —

> " Raise the light, my page, that I may see her —
> Thou art come at last then, haughty Queen !
> Long I've waited, long I've fought my fever :
> Late thou comest, cruel thou hast been."

And the haunting couplet —

> " What voices are these on the clear night air ?
> What lights in the court ? what steps on the stair ? "

The story of Tristram and the two Iseults — the Iseult
he loved and the Iseult he married — has been also

versified by Mr. Swinburne, who treats it with less restraint. In Mr. Arnold's hands it is not so much interesting or complete in itself as the opportunity for stringing together some beauties of melody and niceties of phrase. Such lines as —

> " Above the din her voice is in my ears —
>   I see her form glide through the crossing spears,"

can never be forgotten.

Memorable also is the blank verse —

> "She seems one dying in a mask of youth."

But it may be safely said of this poem that no one has ever read it, or ever will read it for the story, which indeed is rather suggested than told. It is a curious fact that in the first edition of "Tristram and Iseult" the place of King Marc's court was made a dactyl. It runs —

> " Where the prince whom she must wed
>   Keeps his court in Tyntăgel."

It is, of course, Tyntägel, and in later editions the second line became —

> " Dwells on proud Tyntagel's hill."

In every other line where the name occurs a similar change was made.

Among the miscellaneous poems published with "Empedocles," "On the Rhine" is chiefly remarkable for the pretty lines —

> "Eyes too expressive to be blue,
>   Too lovely to be grey."

But " Parting " belongs to a much higher class. It is passionate, as Mr. Arnold's poetry so seldom is, and

it is wholly beautiful, with a rush and swing unusual
in the apostle of philosophic calm, who desired, like
the poor "Independent Preacher," to be at one with
nature —

> "But on the stairs what voice is this I hear,
> Buoyant as morning, and as morning clear?
> Say, has some wet bird-haunted English lawn
> Lent it the music of its trees at dawn?
> Or was it from some sun-fleck'd mountain-brook
> That the sweet voice its upland clearness took?"

This is exquisite melody, and the antistrophe,
beginning —

> "But who is this, by the half-open'd door?"

is quite as good. The poem belongs to a collection
afterwards called "Switzerland," of whom a lady called
Marguerite is the subject. She can hardly have
been a creature of the imagination, but there is no
trace of her identity. Another of the series, called
"Absence," is familiar for the pathetic verses —

> "But each day brings its petty dust
> Our soon-chok'd souls to fill,
> And we forget because we must
> And not because we will."

The lines especially addressed to Marguerite end
with five words —

> "The unplumb'd, salt, estranging sea,"

which can hardly be surpassed for curious felicity in
the English, if in any language. "Self-Dependence"
is a characteristic exhortation to seek refuge from
human troubles in the example of nature. We are
invited to contemplate the stars and the sea —

> " Unaffrighted by the silence round them,
>   Undistracted by the sights they see,
> These demand not that the things without them
>   Yield them love, amusement, sympathy."

The verses are pretty. But, as Gibbon said of
Sulpicius' letter to Cicero, such consolations never
dried a single tear. "The Buried Life" is so perfect,
so finished, and so self-contained, that it would only
be spoiled by quotation. It is, in fact, a variation of
the old theme so finely expressed by Seneca —

> " Illi mors gravis incubat
>   Qui, notus nimis omnibus,
>   Ignotus moritur sibi."

" A Farewell," on the other hand, which belongs to
the Marguerite series, is much less equal, but two of
its stanzas are conspicuously excellent —

> "And though we wear out life, alas !
>   Distracted as a homeless wind,
> In beating where we must not pass,
>   In seeking what we shall not find ;

> "Yet we shall one day gain, life past,
>   Clear prospect o'er our being's whole ;
> Shall see ourselves, and learn at last
>   Our true affinities of soul."

The "Stanzas in Memory of the Author of *Obermann*"
are as much about Goethe as about Senancour; and
Goethe, though the prophet of Matthew Arnold as
well as of Carlyle, belonged to the eighteenth century
rather than the nineteenth. The unrhymed lyric
called "Consolation" is, I confess, beyond me —

> " And countless beings
>   Pass countless moods,"

may be poetry, but it is poetry which I cannot distinguish from prose; and when "two young, fair lovers" cry, "Destiny prolong the present! Time! stand still here!" I can only think of the immortal prayer —

> " Ye gods, annihilate both space and time
> And make two lovers happy."

It is strange indeed to turn from these craggy and spasmodic utterances to the lovely "Lines written in Kensington Gardens" —

> "Calm Soul of all things! make it mine
> To feel, amid the city's jar,
> That there abides a peace of thine,
> Man did not make, and cannot mar."

Not Lucan, not Virgil, only Wordsworth, has more beautifully expressed the spirit of Pantheism.

"The Youth of Nature" and "The Youth of Man" are again neither one thing nor the other. "The Youth of Nature" is not otherwise remarkable than as it exaggerates the Conservatism of Wordsworth, who was very much of a Radical in his early days, as the "Prelude," not published in his lifetime, shows. "The Youth of Man" contains the line —

> " Perfumes the evening air,"

which those may scan who have the power, and those may like who scan. Written as prose, "And they remember with piercing untold anguish the proud boasting of their youth," is well enough. But metrically arranged, it belongs to no metre under Heaven. "And the mists of delusion, and the scales of habit, fall away from their eyes," is irreproachable prose, but impossible

oetry. "Morality," which follows, is a most refresh-
g contrast, and begins at once with a fine stanza —

> " We cannot kindle when we will
>   The fire that in the heart resides ;
>   The spirit bloweth and is still,
>   In mystery our soul abides :
>   But tasks in hours of insight will'd
>   Can be through hours of gloom fulfill'd."

This manly and dignfied tone, so characteristic of
atthew Arnold, is the source of much of his influ-
ace. "Progress," an eloquent expression of his belief
 purely spiritual religion, apart from all creeds and
ogmas, was much altered in later editions. Some of
e changes are certainly improvements. One, I
ink, can hardly be so considered. In the first
ition we read —

> " Quench then the altar fires of your old Gods !
>   Quench not the fire within ! "

his became —

> " Leave then the Cross as ye have left carved gods,
>   But guard the fire within ! "

Here the antithesis disappears, and so the expres-
on becomes weaker. The tribute to all religions,
hristian and other, is a very fine one —

> " Which has not taught weak wills how much they can,
>   Which has not fall'n on the dry heart like rain ?
>   Which has not cried to sunk, self-weary man,
>   ' Thou must be born again ' ? "

he volume ended with an unrhymed piece called
The Future," beginning with the line —

> " A wanderer is man from his birth,"

which to my ear has two superfluous syllables, and ending with the really beautiful verse —

" Murmurs and scents of the infinite Sea."

But it is not by these metrical or unmetrical experiments that Matthew Arnold lives.

Empedocles on Etna, and Other Poems, by " A.," was withdrawn immediately after publication. I was soon, however, followed, in 1853, by a new volume of poems, with the author's name on the title page, and containing many pieces already published besides nine which were new. "Empedocles" itself did not reappear, for reasons stated in the Preface. This essay expresses for the first time Mr. Arnold's conception of poetry, and must be regarded as an epoch in his life. After declaring that he had not withdrawn " Empedocles " because the subject was too remote from the present time, for that he held to be an invalid objection, he thus proceeds :—

" What then are the situations, from the representation of which, though accurate, no poetical enjoyment can be derived ? They are those in which the suffering finds no vent in action; in which a continuous state of mental distress is prolonged, unrelieved by incident, hope, or resistance ; in which there is everything to be endured, nothing to be done. In such situations there is inevitably something morbid, in the description of them something monotonous. When they occur in actual life, they are painful, not tragic; the representation of them in poetry is painful also.

" To this class of situations, poetically faulty as it appears to me, that of Empedocles, as I have endeavoured to represent him, belongs ; and I have

herefore excluded the Poem from the present collec-
on."

This important Preface was Mr. Arnold's earliest
publication in prose. It is written in his best and
purest style, free from the mannerisms and affectations
which did so much in later days to spoil the enjoy-
ent of his readers. But unless Mr. Arnold intended
to suggest that Empedocles fell into the crater by
accident, which is hardly conceivable, the theory does
not quite fit the facts. Suicide is as much action as
murder, and is as capable of dramatic treatment. The
thinness of the boundary between the sublime and
something quite different is a topic more relevant to
voluntary cremation, following a lengthy philosophic
song upon a harp. When Mr. Arnold goes on to ask
and to answer the question what are the eternal objects
 poetry, he is at his best: —

"The Poet, then, has in the first place to select an
excellent action; and what actions are the most excel-
ent? Those, certainly, which most powerfully appeal
 the great primary human affections: to those elemen-
ry feelings which subsist permanently in the race,
and which are independent of time."

That is full of instruction, for ever memorable, and
profoundly true. If Mr. Browning had borne it in
mind, all his poetry would be, as his best poetry is, a
permanent addition to the imaginative literature of
the world. In these pages, thoroughly characteristic of
the writer, appears one phrase which became familiar
within a few years to all Mr. Arnold's readers. The
Greeks, he says, are "the unapproached masters of the
grand style." Professor Saintsbury complains that he
never defined what he meant by the grand style. But

was it necessary ? The words are clear enough, an·
certainly intelligible to all classical scholars. Th·
Greeks, says Mr. Arnold, kept style in the righ·
degree of prominence. They suited, as Hamlet put·
it, the word to the action, the action to the word. ·
am not, however, sure that he exhausts the matte·
when he adds that their range of subjects was so lim·
ited, because so few subjects are excellent. Anothe·
reason was that a story for dramatic representatio·
before the Athenian people must be one which th·
Athenian people knew. They would have resented a·
a dangerous innovation a mere fancy of the dramatist'·
But it must not be too recent, and touch too tende·
a place, as Phrynichus discovered to his cost when h·
was fined for his tragedy on the taking of Miletu·
Most interesting is the passage in which Mr. Arnol·
traces the influence upon modern English poetry o·
Shakespeare's inexhaustible eloquence. This, he think·
encouraged those who came after Shakespeare, an·
regarded him as the greatest of all models, to thin·
too much of expression and too little of compositior·
As the chief example of this error he takes Keat·
and especially "Isabella." He does not depreciat·
Keats, or even "Isabella." On the contrary, he say·
that "this one short poem contains, perhaps, a greate·
number of happy single expressions which one coul·
quote than all the extant tragedies of Sophocles,·
which seems to me a preposterous overstatement. Bu·
he accuses him of subordinating the essential to th·
accidental. That is too large a conclusion to deduc·
from a single poem. It would not be borne out b·
the Sonnets, by the Odes, or by Hyperion. As fo·
Shakespeare himself, it is mere idolatry to preten·

that all he wrote was equally good. There is much
bombast in his early work, and over-expression was
always his besetting sin. It seems a fault in him,
because he was so great. But his inferior contemporaries had it in a much greater degree. It was the
vice of the age rather than of the man. He had at
his best "the severe and scrupulous self-restraint of
the ancients," which Mr. Arnold denies him. But he
had it not always, as they had, and it is true, therefore, that he is a "less safe model." "I know not
how it is," says Mr. Arnold, with insight and felicity
— "I know not how it is, but their commerce with the
ancients appears to me to produce, in those who constantly practise it, a steadying and composing effect
upon their judgment, not of literary works only, but
of men and events in general. They are like persons
who have had a very weighty and impressive experience : they are more truly than others under the empire
of facts, and more independent of the language current
among those with whom they live." That is admirably
said, and it is the last word.

One is rather surprised to find the author of this
luminous Essay, in a letter to his sister, dated the
14th of April 1853, comparing *Villette* unfavourably
with *My Novel*. For though Bulwer was a brilliant
novelist, and is now, perhaps, too much neglected,
there is more genius in the pages of *Villette* than in all
the books he ever wrote. But the letter contains also
an announcement of much interest. "I am occupied,"
he says, "with a thing that gives me more pleasure
than anything I have ever done yet, which is a good
sign ; but whether I shall not ultimately spoil it by
being obliged to strike it off in fragments instead of

at one heat I cannot quite say." He certainly did not spoil it. For the thing was "Sohrab and Rustum," which all admirers of Matthew Arnold would put in the front rank of his poems. It appeared for the first time in 1853; and though Clough "remained in suspense whether he liked it or not," no work of its author's has more genuine beauty. Lord John Russell, who, in his dry fashion, was a sound judge of good literature, had already pronounced Mr. Arnold to be "the one rising young poet of the present day," but his fame really began with the publication of this his third volume. "Sohrab and Rustum" is a story of Central Asia, or, as we used to say, Asia Minor, told in blank verse, and in the Homeric vein. It is called "An Episode," and begins in character with the word "And." Far more truly Homeric than Clough's jolting hexameters, it is as good a specimen of Homer's manner as can be found in English. Rustum is a barbarian, though not an undignified barbarian. But the gentle and sympathetic character of Sohrab is one of the best and most delicate that Matthew Arnold ever drew. That he falls by the hand of his unconscious father is the simple tragedy of the piece. Very noble is his reply to the still sceptical Rustum —

> "Truth sits upon the lips of dying men,
>   And Falsehood, while I liv'd, was far from mine."

And when Rustum, at last convinced that he has slain his son, prays that the Oxus may drown him, Sohrab replies, in the exquisite lines —

> "'Desire not that, my father; thou must live.
>   For some are born to do great deeds, and live,
>   As some are born to be obscur'd, and die.

> Do thou the deeds I die too young to do,
> And reap a second glory in thine age.' "

"The Church of Brou" is chiefly valuable for its beautiful conclusion in heroic verse, beginning —

> "So rest, for ever rest, O Princely Pair !
> In your high Church, 'mid the still mountain air."

The church, however, is not in the mountains, but in the treeless, waterless Burgundian plains. The story is not interesting, nor otherwise well told. The lovely stanzas called "Requiescat" ("Strew on her roses, roses") is perhaps as familiar as anything that Matthew Arnold wrote. This perfect little lyric is worthily rendered into Greek Elegiacs in "Arundines Cami." "The Scholar Gipsy," though it specially appeals through its topography and atmosphere to Oxford men, is dear also to all lovers of poetry. The quaint and fantastic tale, first told by Glanvil, of the young Oxford student who was forced by poverty to leave Oxford and herd with the gipsies, is told again by a lover of the district, the most beautiful in the English midlands. The objection that the poem is too topographical seems to me irrelevant. No one quarrels with Burns for describing Ayrshire, and the scenery of "The Scholar Gipsy" is as familiar as their own homes to thousands of educated Englishmen. The poem is not one from which detached passages can easily be quoted.

> "Sad Patience, too near neighbour to Despair,"

is very close to Shelley.

> "Still nursing the unconquerable hope,
>   Still clutching the inviolable shade,

> With a free onward impulse brushing through,
>   By night, the silver'd branches of the glade,"

are lines which, for a sort of magical charm, have
seldom been surpassed. Fine as they are themselves,
the last two stanzas of "The Scholar Gipsy" are a
little out of place.

> " The young light-hearted Masters of the waves,"

is a line one would not willingly lose. But the
elaborate simile of the "grave Tyrian trader" and
the "merry Grecian coaster" is a less fitting end
than the melancholy contrast between the scholar's
blissful simplicity and our mental strife. The stanzas
in "Memory of the late Edward Quillinan, Esq.," a
forgotten poet, remembered, if at all, as Wordsworth's
son-in-law, and the translator of Camoens, are rather a
copy of verses than a poem.

In 1855 appeared *Poems by Matthew Arnold*, second
series. Of these, two only, "Balder Dead" and
"Separation," were new. By this time, though his
popularity was not wide, his reputation was assured.
Reviewers had begun to treat him with respect,
though there was one curious exception. Writing on
the 3rd of August 1854 to Mr. Wyndham Slade, he
adds this postscript: "My love to J. D. C., and tell
him that the limited circulation of the *Christian
Remembrancer*, makes the unquestionable viciousness of
his article of little importance. I am sure he will be
gratified to think that it is so." After Mr. Arnold's
death, Lord Coleridge, in obvious allusion to this
incident, said that the article in the *Christian Remembrancer*, of which he afterwards bitterly repented,

did not make the slightest difference in the warmth of
a lifelong friendship. Mr. Arnold was, indeed, as
nearly incapable of resentment as a human creature
can be. He was endowed with one of those perfect
tempers which are of more value that many fortunes.
"Balder Dead" is, like "Sohrab and Rustum,"
Homeric in tone, although the subject is taken from
the Norse mythology. It has not the human interest
of the earlier poem. Balder, though he died, was a
god, and the whole machinery is supernatural. A
Frenchman would have said that Mr. Arnold had
accomplished a *tour de force*, and obtained a *succès
d'estime*. Nevertheless, "Balder Dead" is full of
beauty, the verse is musical as well as stately, and
the mourning of nature for "Balder," believed to be
invulnerable, but slain by a stratagem, is admirably
described. Some passages in it are purely Greek, as,
for instance, this speech of Balder —

> "Hermod the nimble, gild me not my death !
> Better to live a serf, a captured man,
> Who scatters rushes in a master's hall,
> Than be a crown'd king here, and rule the dead."

> "ἐν πᾶσιν νεκύεσσι καταφθιμένοισιν ἀνάσσειν."

While the line about "the northern Bear" —

> "And is alone not dipt in Ocean's stream,"

is exactly the beautiful —

> "οἴη δ' ἄμμορός ἐστι λοετρῶν ὠκεανοῖο."

"Balder Dead" must always be a poem for the few.
But it will have readers who enjoy it intensely, even
though they feel that it lacks the peculiar fascination

E

of "Sohrab and Rustum." "Separation," afterwards
included in "Faded Leaves," has a tenderness and a
depth of feeling quite foreign to academic exercises
like "Balder Dead." It comes, like the songs of
Burns, straight from the heart, and the last stanza,
though not faultless in form, is indescribably pathetic: —

> "Then, when we meet, and thy look strays toward me,
>   Scanning my face and the changes wrought there :
> *Who*, let me say, *is this Stranger regards me*,
>   *With the grey eyes, and the lovely brown hair?*"

The effect of the word "Stranger" could only have
been produced by the art which conceals itself, and
appears as simplicity.

On the 17th of February 1856, **Mr.** Arnold wrote to
his sister that he had been elected at the Athenæum,
and looked forward with "rapture" to the use of the
library. One of the first books he read in it seems to
have been the new volume of Ruskin's *Modern Painters*,
upon which he passed, on the 31st of March, this
singular judgment: "Full of excellent *aperçus*, as
usual, but the man and character too febrile, irritable,
and weak to allow him to possess the *ordo concate-
natioque veri*." How he would have laughed at this
pedantry if it had come from a Positivist.

CHAPTER V

THE OXFORD CHAIR

On the 5th of May 1857, Mr. Arnold was elected by Convocation to the Professorship of Poetry at Oxford. His unsuccessful competitor was the Reverend John Ernest Bode, author of *Ballads from Herodotus,* and a thoroughly orthodox divine. It is a curious fact, illustrating the difference between ancient and modern Oxford, that all Mr. Arnold's predecessors in the chair were clergymen. All his successors have been laymen. The Professorship was founded in 1808. The emoluments were trifling, not more than a hundred pounds a year. On the other hand, the duties were not heavy, while the statutory obligation to lecture in Latin, to which Milman and Keble were subject, had been removed. His inaugural lecture was, however, severely classical in tone. Its subject was "The Modern Element in Literature," and in it Mr. Arnold dwelt upon the close intellectual sympathy between Greece in the days of Pericles and the England of his own day. Both ages, he said, demanded intellectual deliverance, and obtained it from literature, especially from poetry. Thus, comparing the Periclean with the Elizabethan age, he showed how much more modern a historian was Thucydides than Raleigh. But the writers most akin to our own were, he contended, the Greek dramatic poets, especially Sophocles and Aristo-

phanes. Latin poetry, being essentially imitative, did
not interpret the time as Greek poetry did. This lecture was not published till February 1869, when it
appeared in *Macmillan's Magazine*. It was followed
by others on the same subject, which have never been
published at all. Although Mr. Arnold retained his
Professorship for ten years, he disliked, as is well
known, the title of Professor. It classed him, as he
plaintively remarked, with Professor Pepper of the
Polytechnic, Professor Anderson, " The Wizard of the
North," and other great men with whom he could not
aspire to rank. He never as Professor resided in Oxford. He wished to be considered a man of letters and
of the world, provided with an honourable and advan-
tageous platform from which to expound his ideas.

The real inauguration of Mr. Arnold's Professorship
was his tragedy called " Merope," which appeared in
1858 with an elaborate and justificatory Preface. In
this Mr. Arnold described England as the stronghold of
the romantic school, and renewed the plea for classical
principles which he had put forward in the Introduction to his Collected Poems. The story of Merope,
the widowed queen of Messenia, whose son Æpytus
avenges upon Polyphontes the murder of Cresphontes,
his father, was well known to antiquity. Aristotle
cites as specially dramatic the scene where Merope is
on the point of killing Æpytus, not recognising him
for her son, but believing him to be her son's destroyer.
Euripides made it the subject of a play, but only a few
fragments have come down to us. Maffei, Voltaire, and
Alfieri successively dramatised it, altering it more or
less to suit modern taste. Mr. Arnold adhered more
strictly to the authority, such as it is, of Hyginus, but

omitted, as too revolting, the marriage of Merope with
Polyphontes, who slew her husband. He seems to
have forgotten that this was an incident in the greatest of all plays, and that the master of human nature
had not shrunk from presenting Gertrude as the wife
of Claudius. This Preface contains an attack upon
French Alexandrines, which is quite unnecessary, and
a criticism of Voltaire as a playwright which is a
little out of place, though the comparison with Racine
is good. But by far the best part of it is that which
describes, with admirable brevity and clearness, the
rise of the Greek drama. No one save Aristotle has
explained in fewer words, or with more picturesque
lucidity, the growth of the complete play from the
chorus and the messenger. The chorus was originally
part of the audience to whom the narrative was
addressed, though they were the only part of the
audience who ventured to interrupt. "The lyrical
element," as Mr. Arnold well says, "was a relief and
solace in the stress and conflict of the action," like
the comic scenes which, as Coleridge observed, Shakespeare interposed after great tragic events. Mr.
Arnold's ideas were excellent. It was in carrying
them out that he failed. To criticise "Merope" is
to dissect a corpse. ψυχάριον εἶ βάσταζον νεκρὸν, would
be a better motto than φιλοκαλοῦμεν μετ' εὐτελείας,
which is the actual one. In vain does Mr. Arnold
make Polyphontes a wise and strong king, endeavour-
ing by years of virtuous rule to expiate the crime into
which ambition has betrayed him. He does not excite
our interest, nor does Merope, nor Æpytus, nor any
of them. The imitation is very skilful. "Merope"
is far more strictly Greek in tone and style than

"Atalanta in Calydon," which is not really Greek at
all. But it has not the sweep, the ring, the melody,
nor the sensuous beauty of that fascinating, though
irregular drama. It is the form without the spirit,
the body without the soul. "Merope" purports to be
a Greek play in English dress. It is really a prize
poem of inordinate length. Mr. Arnold himself hoped
great things from it. "I must read 'Merope' to you,"
he says in a letter to Mrs. Forster of the 25th of July
1857. "I think and hope it will have what Buddha
called the character of *Fixity*, that true sign of the
Law." But literature is not law, and requires something more than fixity, something, as Carlyle would
say, quite other than fixity. "Merope" had a kind
of success, and not the kind which the author least
valued. Dr. Temple, the new Headmaster of Rugby,
an excellent judge, admired it. So did George Henry
Lewes, so did Kingsley, and so, with some reserva-
tions upon the choice of a subject, did Froude. It
even sold well. But the general public never took to
it, and few competent critics would now, I think, say
that they were wrong. There are good lines here and
there, such as the gnome —

"For tyrants make man good beyond himself,"

and the thoroughly Greek antithesis —

"Thy crown condemns thee, while thy tongue absolves,"

and the characteristic couplets —

"To hear another tumult in these streets,
    To have another murder in these halls."

"So rule, that as thy father thou be loved ;
    So rule, that as thy foe thou be obey'd."

But the unrhymed choruses are harsh almost beyond belief, as, for instance —

> "She led the way of death.
> And the plain of Tegea,
> And the grave of Orestes —
> Where, in secret seclusion
> Of his unreveal'd tomb,
> Sleeps Agamemnon's unhappy,
> Matricidal, world-famed,
> Seven-cubit-statured son —
> Sent forth Echemus, the victor, the king."

Perhaps the best of the choric lines are the following, which express one of Mr. Arnold's favourite ideas : —

> "Yea, and not only have we not explored
> That wide and various world, the heart of others,
> But even our own heart, that narrow world
> Bounded in our own breast, we hardly know,
> Of our own actions dimly trace the causes."

But how heavy and lifeless are these verses compared with the simple stanza in "Parting" —

> "Far, far from each other
> Our spirits have grown ;
> And what heart knows another ?
> Ah ! who knows his own ? "

Mr. Arnold was anxious that "Merope" should be known to Robert Browning, whose "Fragment of a Hippolytus," that is, "Artemis Prologises," he justly admired. But Mr. Browning, as we have seen, had the good taste to prefer "Empedocles," with which "Merope" was republished in 1885. Mr. Arnold considered Mrs. Browning as "hopelessly confirmed in her aberration from health, nature, beauty, and truth."

The judgment was severe, but at this distance of time
one can hardly say that it was unsound. What Mr.
Arnold failed to see was that in these forced experiments he ran no small danger of the same kind himself

At the beginning of 1858, nearly seven years after
his marriage, Mr. Arnold took a small house in Chester
Square, and for the first time acquired a settled home.
Both he and his wife were fortunately fond of travel
ling. But his incessant movements as Inspector had
more than satisfied the taste, and they were glad to
have a fixed abode. Mr. Arnold, however, still con
tinued his official tours, and on the 29th of October
1858 he heard John Bright speak at Birmingham.
"He is an orator of almost the highest rank — voice
and manner excellent; perhaps not quite flow enough
— not that he halts or stammers, but I like to have
sometimes more of a *rush* than he ever gives you. He
is a far better speaker than Gladstone." That a "far
better speaker than Gladstone" should not be an orator of the highest rank is a strange paradox. Other
wise the description is excellent, and the comparative
merits of the two speakers will always divide opinion.

Our feelings, says a poet not unlike Matthew Arnold
though inferior to him —

> "Our feelings lose poetic flow
> Soon after twenty-seven or so."

When Mr. Arnold became Professor of Poetry, he was
thirty-four, and his creative work as a poet was almost
finished. In quality some of his later poems are
exquisite. But the quantity of them is very small
Perhaps the critical faculty superseded the poetical
one. He himself said that the critic should keep out

of the region of immediate practice. But his first published work in prose was a political pamphlet. It appeared in 1859 with the title *England and the Italian Question*, and a motto from the Vulgate, *Sed nondum est finis*, — "But the end is not yet." This pamphlet, never republished, and now very scarce, is a philosophical argument for the freedom and independence of Italy. It contains some curiously bad prophecies, such as that Alsace must always be French, and that Prussia could not take the field against either Austria or France. But the historical argument for Italy is strong, and well put. Mr. Arnold shows that Italy was independent of a foreign yoke throughout the fourteenth and fifteenth centuries. His Liberalism, however, was always moderate, being, in fact, Whiggery; and when he comes forward as the champion of Italian nationality, he is careful to disclaim all sympathy with such inferior races as the Hungarians, the Irish, and the Poles. In the true Whig spirit, which Mr. Arnold may have imbibed from Lord Lansdowne, is his eulogy of the English aristocracy, and the governing skill they had displayed since the Revolution of 1688.

When Mr. Arnold praised the disinterestedness of France, he did not foresee the annexation of Savoy and Nice, which followed next year, having really been arranged before the war between the Emperor Napoleon and Count Cavour. Victor Emmanuel obtained for Italy Lombardy and the central Italian Provinces, except Venetia and the Papal States. The inhabitants of Nice and Savoy voted by overwhelming majorities for incorporation with France, but it can hardly be said with truth that Louis Napoleon's policy was disin-

terested. The opportunity of observing public opinion
in France on the war was given to Mr. Arnold by his
appointment, in January 1859, as Foreign Assistant
Commissioner on Education to visit France, Holland,
Belgium, Switzerland, and Piedmont. " I cannot tell
you," he wrote to his sister, Miss Arnold, " how much
I like the errand, and, above all, to have the French
district." Holland he did not appreciate, and he pronounced the Belgians to be the most contemptible people in Europe. But France he thoroughly enjoyed,
especially Paris, where he was always at home. At
Paris he " had a long and very interesting conversation
with Lord Cowley *tête-à-tête* for about three-quarters of
an hour the other day. . . . He entirely shared my
conviction as to the French always beating any number of Germans who come into the field against
them " (*Letters*, vol. i. p. 96). Such are the pro-
phetic powers of exalted diplomatists. In this same
letter Mr. Arnold refers to that political classic,
" Mill on Liberty," in language of very chastened
enthusiasm. " It is," he says, " worth reading at-
tentively, being one of the few books that incul-
cate tolerance in an unalarming and inoffensive
way." At Paris also Mr. Arnold met Prosper Mérimée,
and dined with Sainte-Beuve. He was much amused
to find himself described as " Monsieur le Professeur
Docteur Arnold, Directeur-Général de toutes les Écoles
de la Grande Bretagne," which is certainly a compre-
hensive title.

On Mr. Arnold's return to England he joined the
Queen's Westminster Volunteers; and it is strange to
read in a letter to his sister, dated the 21st of November 1859, a refutation of the long since obsolete argu-

ment that it was dangerous to arm the people. "The bad feature in the proceeding," he says, "is the hideous English toadyism with which lords and great people are invested with the commands in the corps they join, quite without respect of any consideration of their efficiency. This proceeds from our national bane — the immense vulgar-mindedness, and, so far, real inferiority of the English middle classes." It is important in these years, before Mr. Arnold took up definitely the business of a critic, to watch the development of his literary opinions. There was always something antipathetic to him in Tennyson. "The fault I find with Tennyson" (he wrote, on the 17th of December 1860, about the *Idylls of the King*), "is that the peculiar charm and aroma of the Middle Age he does not give in them." That, I think, would be generally admitted. Much more disputable is what follows. "The real truth is [always a suspicious beginning] that Tennyson, with all his temperament and artistic skill, is deficient in intellectual power." After all, he wrote *In Memoriam*. Matthew Arnold, despite his Sonnet, did not share the national idolatry of Shakespeare. Compared with Homer, he was imperfection to perfection.

Like most of the upper and middle classes at the time, Mr. Arnold completely misjudged the situation in America at the outbreak of the Civil War. On the 28th of January 1861 he wrote to Mrs. Forster: "I have not much faith in the nobility of nature of the Northern Americans. I believe they would consent to any compromise sooner than let the Southern States go. However, I believe the latter mean to go, and think they will do better by going, so the baseness

of the North will not be tempted too strongly." Mrs.
Forster's husband took a juster view.

In 1861 appeared, first as a Parliamentary Blue
Book, and afterwards as an independent volume, Mr.
Arnold's *Popular Education in France, with Notices of
that of Holland and Switzerland.* The Introduction,
which alone has much interest now, was republished
nearly twenty years afterwards in *Mixed Essays,* and
called "Democracy." It is a State paper of great
value and importance. Mr. Arnold was always a keen
critic of his own countrymen. He had learned from
his father's eloquent and dignified *Lectures on Modern
History,* that to flatter a great nation like England
was to insult her, and that it was part of true patriotism to tell her of her faults. In this paper, written
with the admirable simplicity that always distinguished his style, and without the mannerisms that
afterwards disfigured it, he argues that the English
dread of interference by the State, formerly natural
and reasonable, had become irrational and obsolete.
An aristocratic executive, he contended, was inclined
to govern as little as possible, and such an executive
England had hitherto possessed. But with the spread
of democratic ideas, which he observed with the cold
but appreciative sympathy of a Whig, and the enlarge-
ment of the franchise, which he clearly foresaw, there
would, he thought, be more need and less repugnance
for the action of the Government. He cites the example of France, where the "common people," or, as we
should say, the masses, were in his opinion superior to
our own. The moral he drew was, of course, the necessity of public teaching, organised by the State. No
other would have been relevant to his subject. Yet

it is remarkable that the schools which he recommended were not those elementary establishments set up ten years later by his brother-in-law, but the secondary schools of France. He endeavoured therefore to combat the jealousy of the State which pervaded the middle classes, and to prove that they required its aid in bringing order out of chaos. Admitting that there was too much government in France, he urged that there was too little in England, and as an Englishman he pleaded for more. High reason and fine culture were, he said, the great objects for which the nation should strive. He lamented the decline of aristocratic culture, of which the fine flower in the eighteenth century was Lord Carteret. But culture, except so far as it involves leisure, has nothing to do with class, and Lord Carteret was a wholly exceptional man. If Mr. Arnold had taken the Lord Derby of his own day, and compared him with the Duke of Newcastle in Lord Carteret's time, or if he had contrasted Mr. Gladstone with Sir Robert Walpole, the result would have been very different. But this is by the way. Mr. Arnold's main principle in this excellent essay is perfectly sound; and though popular education did not develop itself in the precise form he expected, a deep debt of gratitude is due to him for the interest he aroused in its progress.

In 1861 Mr. Arnold published his three lectures " On translating Homer," followed the next year by a fourth on the same subject called " Last Words." These most interesting and valuable discourses have been the delight of all scholars ever since they appeared. They are among the author's most characteristic productions, showing even for the first time that tendency to the undue repetition of words and phrases which afterwards became a vice of his style. From one of Mr. Arnold's main conclusions I respectfully, and in good company, dissent. I cannot think that the English hexameter is the best metre for a translation of Homer. The English hexameter is an exotic, which does not flourish in our soil. Occasional instances to the contrary may be quoted from Longfellow's "Evangeline" and from Kingsley's "Andromeda" —

"Chanting the hundredth Psalm, that grand old Puritan anthem,"

which is Longfellow's, and

"As when an osprey aloft, dock-eyebrowed, royally crested,"

which is Kingsley's, are perfect. But such successes cannot be maintained. So far as I know, the one example to the contrary in the English language is Dr. Hawtrey's famous translation from the third book of the *Iliad*, beginning

"Clearly the rest I behold of the dark-eyed sons of Achaia,"

and ending

"There in their own dear land, their fatherland, Lacedæmon."

Mr. Arnold's own specimens do not rise much above mediocrity, and he must have been misled by personal friendship when he compared Clough's clever versemaking with the simple dignity of Homer. We may feel then that Mr. Arnold was right when he declined the proposal to translate Homer himself, and yet be supremely grateful to him for having dealt in so luminous a manner with the general principles of translation. He was unfortunately led by the accidents of

time and place, or perhaps by the spirit of mockery,
to bestow too much notice upon a very bad translation
of Homer made by a very learned man. Mr. Francis
Newman of Balliol, brother of the celebrated Cardinal,
though eccentric in many ways, never did anything
more eccentric than his translation of the *Iliad*, which,
but for Mr. Arnold, would have died almost as soon as
it was born. Pope, on the other hand, Mr. Arnold dismisses with Bentley's scornful dictum, for which Pope
put him in the "Dunciad," that it was a pretty poem,
but not Homer. It is certainly not Homer, for the
very good reason that Pope knew little or no Greek.
But it is much more than a pretty poem, and it will
never cease to be read. Such lines as —

> "Let tyrants govern with an iron rod,
>   Oppress, destroy, and be the scourge of God;
>   Since he who like a father held his reign,
>   So soon forgot, was just and mild in vain,"

are imperishable, and no one would wish that they
should perish. Pope's *Iliad* and Pope's *Odyssey* are
great English epics. To Chapman also Mr. Arnold is
less than just. Even if Chapman had not inspired
Keats's immortal Sonnet, the full proud sail of his
great verse would still be the best English equivalent
for the majestic roll of the Greek hexameter.

Mr. Arnold's test of Homeric translation is to ask
how it affects those who both know Greek and can
appreciate poetry, such as Dr. Hawtrey of Eton, Dr.
Thompson of Trinity, and Mr. Jowett of Balliol. Mr.
Arnold rightly finds fault with Mr. Ruskin's fantastic
theory, that in referring to the death of Castor and
Pollux, Homer called the earth in which they lay

"life-giving," because he wished to relieve the gloom
of the picture. Homer called the earth life-giving,
there as elsewhere, because it was a fixed epithet of
the earth. But Mr. Arnold himself is almost as fantastic when he compares Homer with Voltaire because
they are both lucid. Certainly this comparison will
not help the translator "to reproduce on the general
reader, as nearly as possible, the general effect of
Homer." Mr. Arnold believed as passionately as Mr.
Gladstone and Mr. Lang in the unity of Homer, which
Sir Richard Jebb tells us is incredible. "The insur-
mountable obstacle to believing the *Iliad* the consoli-
dated work of several poets is this : that the work
of great masters is unique, and the *Iliad* [he does
not here mention the *Odyssey*] has a great master's
genuine stamp, and that stamp is *the grand style*."
What, then, is the grand style? It "arises in poetry
when a noble nature, poetically gifted, treats with
simplicity or with severity a serious subject." The
Iliad and the *Odyssey* are certainly not what we ourselves mean by ballad-poetry, and attempts like Dr.
Maginn's to translate them into a series of ballads
have always failed. It is a pity that Mr. Arnold
mixed up this wholesome doctrine with the highly
controversial statement, from which his own father
would have been the first to dissent, that Macaulay's
"pinchbeck" *Lays* were "one continual falsetto."
The remark, moreover, is quite irrelevant, for Macaulay never dreamed of imitating Homer. His only
published translation from Homer is in the metre of
Pope, and as unlike the *Lays* as possible.

Homer, says Mr. Arnold, is rapid, plain, simple, and
noble. The great mine of diction for the English

translator of Homer, he adds, is the English Bible. So far, so good. But it is a long way from those premisses to the conclusion that the hexameter should be the form of verse employed. Mr. Arnold's case is here not a strong one. "I know all that is said," he tells us, "against the use of hexameters in English poetry; but it comes only to this, that among us they have not yet been used on any considerable scale with success. *Solvitur ambulando:* this is an objection which can best be met by *producing* good English hexameters." That is not quite all that can be said against the use of hexameters in English. It may also be said that they depend upon quantity, and that English poetry depends upon accent. But taking Mr. Arnold at his word, I cannot think that his own hexameters justify his theory. Here are some of them —

" So shone forth, in front of Troy, by the bed of Xanthus,
  Between that and the ships, the Trojan's numerous fires.
  In the plain there were kindled a thousand fires : by each one
  There sat fifty men, in the ruddy light of the fire :
  By their chariots stood the steeds, and champed the white
      barley,
  While their masters sat by the fire and waited for morning."

The last line is the best, but all are wooden. Compare Tennyson's rendering of the same passage in blank verse —

    " So many a fire between the ships and stream
     Of Xanthus blazed before the towers of Troy,
     A thousand on the plain ; and close by each
     Sat fifty in the blaze of burning fire ;
     And eating hoary grain and pulse the steeds,
     Fixt by their cars, waited the golden dawn."

These verses are far more truly Homeric than Mr. Arnold's limping hexameters. It is the more

F

strange that Mr. Arnold should have rejected the claims of blank verse, because his own " Sohrab and Rustum," to say nothing of " Balder Dead," is especially Homeric. To Worsley's *Odyssey*, which adopts the Spenserian stanza, Mr. Arnold pays in " Last Words " a due tribute of high praise. In this same lecture he alludes to the death of Clough, which he afterwards lamented in verse not unlike that consecrated by Moschus to the death of Bion.

Mr. Arnold's life, which was not an eventful one, can be traced with sufficient clearness from his letters. He thought " Essays and Reviews " a breach of the scriptural rule against putting new wine into old bottles, and had needless fears for their effect upon Dr. Temple's position at Rugby. Nothing has ever been able to keep Dr. Temple back, or to diminish the public respect for his rugged, massive character. Early in 1861 Sainte-Beuve published his volume on Chateaubriand, with a French translation of Matthew Arnold's poem on " Obermann," which naturally gave the author much pleasure. In the same year Mr. Arnold contributed to a volume called *Victoria Regia*, edited by Adelaide Procter, the lovely poem entitled " A Southern Night." These exquisite stanzas were written to commemorate his brother William, who died at Gibraltar on the way back from India in April 1859. The best known, and perhaps the best, lines in it, are those which describe us world-pervading English folk who are ever on the move —

> " And see all sights from pole to pole,
>   And glance and nod and bustle by —
> And never once possess our soul
>   Before we die."

The Revised Code of 1862, in which Mr. Arnold
took a keen, though not a friendly interest, was a
consequence of the Duke of Newcastle's Commission,
appointed the previous year. But it went beyond
the Report of the Commissioners. It was really the
work of Mr. Lowe, the Vice-President of the Council,
and Mr. Lingen, the Secretary to the Department.
Mr. Lowe was, perhaps, the ablest, certainly the
cleverest, man who ever held that important office.
Like Mr. Lingen, he had highly distinguished himself
at Oxford, but his views on the education of the
masses were strictly and exclusively ultilitarian. He
was very clear-headed; he always knew what he
wanted; and though he rather liked flouting popular
prejudices, he had the knack of coining popular phrases.
Taking up a remark of the Commissioners that too
much time was spent in the national schools upon the
performances of prize pupils, while the work of teaching the rudiments to the general mass was propor-
tionately neglected, he proposed a capitation grant,
combined with payment by results. Thus, he said,
if elementary education was not cheap, it would be
efficient; if not efficient, it would be cheap. The
epigram was ingenious, and the phrase " payment by
results " succeeded well. But Mr. Lowe soon found, as
most ministers do find who touch education, that he had
raised a storm. The protests of " born educationalists,"
like Sir James Kay-Shuttleworth and Mr. Arnold,
might have been disregarded. But the Conservative
Opposition, who were very strong in the Parliament
of 1859, took the matter up. They had the Church
of England behind them, and the Revised Code was
itself revised. One-third only of the Government

grant was given for attendance, the remaining two-thirds being awarded only after examination. Thus Mr. Arnold, who had from the first attacked the Revised Code as too mechanical, achieved at least half a victory. He was rather afraid of losing his place for writing against his chiefs. But nothing happened to him, and Mr. Lowe himself had soon afterwards to resign.

The Creweian Oration at Oxford, which accompanies the bestowal of honorary degrees, is delivered alternately by the Public Orator and the Professor of Poetry. It fell to Mr. Arnold's turn in 1862, when Lord Palmerston was made a Doctor of Civil Law. The Prince Consort and Lord Canning had both died within the year, so that there was no lack of topics for this annual exercise in elegant Latinity. But Mr. Arnold did not confine himself to his official work and his Professorial duties. He made a vigorous attack upon Bishop Colenso's book on the Penta-teuch, which gave great offence to many of his Liberal friends. The article was published in *Macmillan's Magazine* for January 1863, with the title "The Bishop and the Philosopher." The Philosopher was Spinoza, with whom few Biblical critics, and certainly not Mr. Arnold himself, could be favourably com-pared. Bishop Colenso's book has long been forgotten, and he himself is remembered rather as the fearless champion of the Zulus than as the corrector of figures in the Mosaic record. Mr. Arnold was, perhaps, needlessly severe when he described the Bishop as eliciting a "titter from educated Europe." But it was true that his arithmetical computations neither edified the many nor informed the few. When

Mr. Disraeli spoke of prelates whose study of theology commenced after they had grasped the crozier, he hit the point. These absurdities and impossibilities in Biblical arithmetic — Colenso's "favourite science," as Mr. Arnold called it — were not new to the learned world. Nor did they affect the questions of believing in God and leading a good life, which Spinoza, a lay saint, considered to be alone essential. In the following number of *Macmillan* Mr. Arnold at once served a friend, and expressed the positive side of his theology, by a sympathetic review of Stanley's *Lectures on the Jewish Church*. On the death of Thackeray, which occurred at the end of this year, Mr. Arnold pronounced him not to be a great writer. This is a judgment which, coming from any one else, Mr. Arnold himself would have called *saugrenu*. If Thackeray was not a great writer, no English novelist was so. *Vanity Fair, Esmond, Barry Lyndon*, and the first volume of *Pendennis* are scarcely to be matched in English fiction.

Although Mr. Arnold was sent abroad to report on primary education only, he also contrived to see some of the best secondary schools in France, and upon his visits to them he founded his treatise on *A French Eton*, which appeared in 1864. The name was not very happily chosen. Mr. Arnold was easily convicted by Mr. Stephen Hawtrey of not understanding the tutorial system at Eton. Nobody understands the tutorial system at Eton except Eton men, and they cannot explain it. But for the rest the book, besides being most agreeably written, is both interesting and important. Mr. Arnold's *French Eton* is the Lyceum at Toulouse, which he rather minutely describes. It is, or was, maintained partly by the State and partly by the Commune. It comprised both day-boys and boarders; there were scholarships open to competition, and, by way of a conscience clause, there was a Protestant minister to conduct the religious teaching of the Protestant pupils. The subjects of tuition, which were the same in all the French Lyceums, differed chiefly from what was then taught at Eton by including science and French grammar. Science is now taught in all the public schools of England. English Grammar is still, I believe, neglected. Nobody made any profit out of these Lyceums, and the terms were therefore much lower than in our public schools, ranging from fifty pounds a boarder to twenty pounds a day-boy. It is a misrepresentation to say that Mr. Arnold compared these French schools, and their too systematic routine, with Eton, or Harrow, or his own Rugby. He contrasted them with the schools available for the less wealthy portion of the middle classes in England, and, in spite of the excellent work since done by the Endowed School Commissioners, he might make the same contrast still. Our secondary education is still the weak point in our teaching, and it was not Mr. Arnold's fault that his timely counsels were neglected.

But the most fascinating part of a delightful book is the account of Lacordaire's private school at Sorrèze. Here the payment was astonishingly small, varying from five to fifteen pounds a year. Of Lacordaire himself, whom, with all his strictness, his pupils did not merely respect but love, Mr. Arnold paints a charming picture, as unlike his father as his conscience would let him. The conclusion he draws from the whole matter is that the law of supply and demand will not suffice for education in the true sense of the word. What made it, according to his view, more efficient in France than in England was first supervision, and secondly publicity. To the familiar maxim that the State had better leave things alone he opposed Burke's definition of the State as beneficence acting by rule. From Burke's political philosophy Mr. Arnold drew most of his own lessons in politics, and, as an inspector of schools appointed by the State, it was natural that he should disbelieve in the sufficiency of private enterprise. So far as elementary education was concerned, he had his way. He lived to see it made compulsory, though not to see it made free. The upper and middle classes were left to educate themselves, or to go uneducated, as they pleased.

CHAPTER VI

ESSAYS IN CRITICISM

Mr. Arnold was, as we have seen, elected Professor of Poetry at Oxford in 1857. The election was for a period of five years, but in accordance with custom he was re-elected for a similar term in 1862. He had more than justified the choice of the university, and his literary reputation was firmly established. At that time Mr. Disraeli was Leader of the Conservative party in the House of Commons, and at the very height of his Parliamentary powers. No politician except Lord Palmerston had then more influence in the country, for Mr. Gladstone's popularity was to come, and Lord Derby's never came. At Aston Clinton, Sir Anthony de Rothschild's house in Buckinghamshire, where he was in the habit of staying, Mr. Arnold met Mr. Disraeli on the 27th of January 1864. Mr. Disraeli was always at his best with men of letters. He sincerely respected them, and was proud to be one of their number. On this occasion he was very gracious to Mr. Arnold. "You have a great future before you," he said, "and you deserve it." He then went on to add that he had given up literature because he was not one of those who could do two things at once, but that he admired most the men like Cicero, who could. Bishop Wilberforce was another guest, and preached the next day a sermon which, in Mr.

Arnold's opinion, showed him to have no "real power of mind." "A truly emotional spirit," Mr. Arnold wrote to his mother, "he undoubtedly has, beneath his outside of society-haunting and men-pleasing, and each of the two lives he leads gives him the more zest for the other." It was clearly the Bishop from whom Mr. Arnold drew the type that "make the best of both worlds." There are probably few who would deny that he correctly estimated "the great lord bishop of England," as Wilberforce's satellites liked to call him, and as he liked to be called. His appreciation of Tennyson, on the other hand, was utterly inadequate. "I do not," he wrote to Mr. Dykes Campbell on the 22nd of September 1864, "I do not think Tennyson a great and powerful spirit in any line, as Goethe was in the line of modern thought, Wordsworth in that of contemplation, Byron even in that of passion; and unless a poet, especially a poet at this time of day, is that, my interest in him is only slight, and my conviction that he will not finally stand high is firm." It is strange that any critic should attribute want of sympathy with modern thought to the author of *In Memoriam*. It is stranger still that he should consider Byron a greater poet than Tennyson. But, for some reason or other, Mr. Arnold did not appreciate his English contemporaries. That reason was certainly not envy or jealousy, for of such feelings he was incapable. As his friend Lord Coleridge said, they "withered in his presence." The prejudice did not apply to foreigners. He idolised Sainte-Beuve. Nor was it strictly confined to contemporaries. He was never just to Shelley, and not till the close of his life to Keats. He seems to have got it into his head that Tennyson was being " run " against Wordsworth, which is the last thing that Tennyson himself would have desired. But it is true that forty years ago Tennyson suffered a good deal from injudicious admirers. His *May Queen,* and *Airy, Fairy Lilian* were extolled as gems of the purest water. Rash, however, as this indiscriminate praise may have been, it should not have prevented Mr. Arnold from admiring *Tithonus.*

Essays in Criticism appeared in 1865. It is Mr. Arnold's most important work in prose, the central book, so to speak, of his life. Although it was not at first widely read, it made an immediate and a profound impression upon competent judges of literature. There had been nothing like it since Hazlitt. There has been nothing like it since. Mr. Arnold's judgments are sometimes eccentric, and the place which he assigns to the two De Guérins is altogether out of proportion. But the value of *Essays in Criticism* does not depend upon this or that isolated opinion expressed by its author. Mr. Arnold did not merely criticise books himself. He taught others how to criticise them. He laid down principles, if he did not always keep the principles he laid down. Nobody, after reading *Essays in Criticism,* has any excuse for not being a critic. Mr. Ruskin once lamented that he had made a great number of entirely foolish people take an interest in art, and if there were too few critics in 1865, there may be too many now. But Mr. Arnold is not altogether responsible for the quantity. He has more to do with the quality, and the quality has beyond question been improved.

The famous Preface to *Essays in Criticism* was in the

second edition, the edition of 1869, curtailed, and, perhaps wisely, shorn of some ephemeral allusions. It contains, as every one knows, the exquisite address to Oxford: "beautiful city, so venerable, so lovely, so unravaged by the fierce intellectual life of our century, so serene." The negative part of this praise could hardly be given now. Even in 1865 Oxford was not quite so free from intellectual disturbances as in Mr. Arnold's undergraduate days. But the question he asked then may be asked still: "And yet, steeped in sentiment as she lies, spreading her gardens to the moonlight, and whispering from her towers the last enchantments of the Middle Age, who will deny that Oxford, by her ineffable charm, keeps ever calling us nearer to the true goal of all of us, to the ideal, to perfection — to beauty, in a word, which is only truth seen from another side, — nearer, perhaps, than all the science of Tübingen?" Of science, in the narrow or physical sense, Mr. Arnold knew little or nothing, and he had not his father's love of history. But of the old Oxford education, *literæ humaniores*, there have been few finer products. Excellent, in a lighter style, is his apology to Mr. Wright, the translator of Homer, for having been too vivacious. "Yes, the world will soon be the Philistines'! and then with every voice, not of thunder, silenced, and the whole earth filled and ennobled every morning by the magnificent roaring of the young lions of the *Daily Telegraph*, we shall all yawn in one another's faces with the dismallest, the most unimpeachable gravity."

For it is in this volume, in his essay on Heine, that Mr. Arnold first uses the word "Philistine," borrowed of course from the German, and it played afterwards

so large a part in his philosophy, that the passage
may as well be quoted in full.

"*Philistinism!* — we have not the expression in
English. Perhaps we have not the word because we
have so much of the thing. At Soli I imagine they
did not talk of Solecisms; and here, at the very
head-quarters of Goliath, nobody talks of Philistinism.
The French have adopted the term *épicier* (grocer), to
designate the sort of being whom the Germans designate by the term Philistine; but the French term —
besides that it casts a slur upon a respectable class,
composed of living and susceptible members, while the
original Philistines are dead and buried long ago — is
really, I think, in itself much less apt and expressive
than the German term. Efforts have been made to
obtain in English some term equivalent to *Philister* or
épicier; Mr. Carlyle has made several such efforts:
'respectability with its thousand gigs,' he says; well,
the occupant of every one of these gigs is, Mr. Carlyle
means, a Philistine. However, this word *respectable*
is far too valuable a word to be thus perverted from
its proper meaning; if the English are ever to have a
word for the thing we are speaking of — and so pro-
digious are the changes which the modern spirit is
introducing, that even we English shall, perhaps, one
day come to want such a word — I think we had much
better take the term *Philistine* itself."

The Philistines should, perhaps, have been introduced to our notice in the first essay, which deals
with the function of criticism. Here, however, we
get another of Mr. Arnold's favourite sentiments, his
worship of Burke. Heaven forbid that I should say a
word against that great man — great in politics, great

in literature, passionate in patriotism, fertile in ideas.
But to the proposition that he was the greatest writer
of English prose I respectfully demur. The greatest
writer of English prose is Shakespeare. I do not
think that Burke wrote as pure English as his com-
patriot Goldsmith, or even as Swift. Eloquent,
massively eloquent, as he can be, he does not in my
judgment rise to the level of Bacon, or Milton, or
Dryden, or Sir Thomas Browne. In this essay, perhaps the best he ever wrote, Mr. Arnold quotes Burke's
"return upon himself" in the *Thoughts on French
Affairs,* as one of the finest things in English literature,
and yet characteristically un-English. Well, Burke
was not an Englishman. He was an Irishman, and
he sometimes indulged in the "blind hysterics of the
Celt." The passage here quoted by Mr. Arnold is a
very fine one, and deserves his panegyric. "If," says
Burke, "a great change is to be made in human
affairs, the minds of men will be fitted to it; the
general opinions and feelings will draw that way.
Every fear, every hope will forward it, and then they
who persist in opposing this mighty current in human
affairs will appear rather to resist the decrees of
Providence itself than the mere designs of men.
They will not be resolute and firm, but perverse
and obstinate." Mr. Arnold, in citing these noble
words, written in December 1791, has fallen into
a strange historical error. He calls these *Thoughts
on French Affairs* "some of the last pages" Burke
"ever wrote." Burke died in 1797. The *Letter to a
Noble Lord* and the three *Letters on a Regicide Peace*
were written in 1796. He was past returning upon
himself then. Except where Ireland was concerned,

the French Revolution had made him incapable of
seeing more than one side to a question. The British
Constitution had always been his idol. He forgot, as
Mr. Goldwin Smith says, that nothing human is sacred.

The first principle of criticism was, said Mr. Arnold,
disinterestedness. This end was to be attained by
"keeping aloof from practice," by a free play of the
mind, and by the avoidance of ulterior considerations,
political, social, or religious. Two of these rules are
negative, as indeed, for that matter, are the Ten Commandments. The third is vague. It is difficult to
believe that Mr. Arnold would have been a worse
critic if he had written more poetry after he was
thirty-five. And he certainly did not agree with
Mark Pattison in holding that the man who wanted
to persuade anybody of anything was not a man of
letters. He was a missionary, almost an apostle, the
antagonist of Philistinism, the champion of sweetness
and light. His own particular criticisms were not
always, to use his own phrase, "of the centre."
His great and distinguishing merit as a critic was
that he had a theory, that he regarded his subject as a
whole, that he could not merely give reasons for his
opinions, but show that they were something more
than opinions, that they were the deliberate judgments
of a trained intelligence working upon a systematic
order of ideas. In this very Essay he contrasts the
disinterestedness of French with the partisanship of
English critcism, and the passage is important, on
more grounds than one. "An organ," he says, "like
the *Revue des Deux Mondes*, having for its main
function to understand and utter the best that is
known and thought in the world, existing, it may be

said, as just an organ for the free play of the mind,
we have not; but we have the *Edinburgh Review*, existing as an organ of the Old Whigs, and for as much
play of the mind as may suit its being that; we have
the *Quarterly Review*, existing as an organ of the Tories,
and for as much play of mind as may suit its being
that; we have the *British Quarterly Review*, existing as
an organ of the political Dissenters, and for as much
play of mind as may suit its being that; we have the
Times, existing as an organ of the common, satisfied,
well-to-do Englishman, and for as much play of mind
as may suit its being that." Even in the great days
of M. Buloz, when the *Revue des Deux Mondes* really
was the first literary organ of Europe, it was too
aristocratic and too orthodox to deserve the praise of
pure intellectual impartiality. But it was true then,
and, with qualifications, it is true now, that French
magazines and newspapers treat literature far more
seriously than our own. What change there has been
since 1865 on this side of the Channel is all for the
better, and is due to no man so much as to Matthew
Arnold. But, as I have said, I quote this passage for
another reason. It is the first conspicuous instance of
a fault which grew upon Mr. Arnold until at last it
almost destroyed the pleasure of reading his prose.
I mean the trick of repetition. Repetition is not
always a vice. Delicately managed by great writers,
it may be a powerful mode of heightening rhetorical
effect. But the art of using without abusing it is a
very difficult, and a very delicate one. Beautiful
examples of it may be found in the Collects of the
English Church. Take, for instance, the Collect for
St. John the Evangelist's Day:—

"Merciful Lord, we beseech thee to cast thy bright beams of light upon thy Church, that it, being enlightened by the doctrine of thy blessed Apostle and Evangelist Saint John, may so walk in the light of thy truth, that it may at length attain to the light of everlasting life; through Jesus Christ our Lord."

Here the repetition of the word "light," with the still more beautiful repetition of the word "charity" in the great chapter of Corinthians, is a real artistic merit.   It charms, and it tells.   But the words "as may suit its being that" have no attraction or distinction of any kind. The first time they occur, one passes them over without much notice.   The fourth time they become almost intolerable.   It is amazing that a man of Mr. Arnold's fastidious taste and true scholarship should not have instinctively avoided so paltry a device.   But the fact is that Mr. Arnold had the gift of seeing his own faults without seeing that they were his own.   His Essay on the *Literary Influence of Academies* is a most brilliant and entertaining one, much better worth reading than Swift's on the same subject.   He attributes to Academies the power of saving nations from the "note of provinciality."   Nowhere is Mr. Arnold's peculiar gift of urbane and humorous persuasiveness better displayed than in his own account of how the French Academy was founded by Richelieu.   He quotes a sentence from Bossuet's panegyric of St. Paul, hardly to be surpassed for eloquence and grandeur.   He contrasts it with some rather coarse specimens of Burke and Jeremy Taylor at their worst.   These, he says, are provincial, Bossuet's prose is prose of the centre. Very likely he is right.   Very likely an academy, if it could not bring us all up to the level of Bossuet,

would have kept great English writers more within
bounds. An English Academy might, as Mr. Arnold
implies, have given Addison more ideas. Joubert
might have had fewer ideas if there had been no
French Academy. Although it seems to me paradoxical, I will not deny it. But then suddenly one lights,
or rather stumbles, upon this sentence. " In short,
where there is no centre like an academy, if you have
genius and powerful ideas, you are apt not to have
the best style going; if you have precision of style
and not genius, you are apt not to have the best ideas
going." Is that " prose of the centre " ? Is it not
rather tricky, flashy, provincial ?

Mr. Arnold's affection for Maurice and Eugénie de
Guérin, that hapless brother and sister who excited
the sympathy of Sainte-Beuve, is almost too gentle
and touching for criticism. And his favourite quotation from Maurice de Guérin's *Centaure* has no doubt a
singular charm. But when it comes to saying that
the talent of this young Frenchman, now almost forgotten in his own country, had "more of distinction
and power than the talent of Keats," the English
reader must feel that if this is to be "central," provinciality has its consolations. But indeed, Mr.
Arnold's reputation would have stood higher if he had
left Keats alone. He cannot even quote him correctly.
Keats did not write, as in the essay on Maurice de
Guérin Mr. Arnold makes him write,

> "moving waters at their priestlike task
> Of *cold* ablution round Earth's human shores."

He wrote *pure* ablution. What a difference! How
tame and awkward is the one; how supremely perfect

G

is the other! Matthew Arnold's avowed master in
criticism was Sainte-Beuve. He could hardly have
had a better. The doctrine of disinterestedness is
undoubtedly Sainte-Beuve's, and may be found at
the beginning of the essay on Mademoiselle de
l'Espinasse: —

"Le critique ne doit point avoir de partialité et n'est
d'aucune côterie. Il n'épouse les gens que par un
temps, et ne fait que traverser les groupes divers sans
s'y enchaîner jamais. Il passe résolument d'un camp
à l'autre; et de ce qu'il a rendu justice d'un côté ce ne
lui est jamais une raison de la refuser à ce qui est
vis-à-vis. Ainsi, tour à tour, il est à Rome ou à
Carthage, tantôt pour Argos et tantôt pour Ilion."
— "The critic ought not to be partial, and has no
set. He takes up people only for a time, and
does no more than pass through different groups
without ever chaining himself down. He passes firmly from one camp to the other; and never, because
he has done justice to one side, refuses the same to
the opposite party. Thus, turn by turn, he is at
Rome and at Carthage, sometimes for Argos, and
sometimes for Troy."

"Tros Tyriusque mihi nullo discrimine agetur."

But if it was to Sainte-Beuve, and not to George
Sand, that Mr. Arnold owed his excessive fondness
for the De Guérins, the benefit was a doubtful one.
They fill, as Mr. Saintsbury says, too large a space in
a volume which contains such subjects as Heine,
Spinoza, and Marcus Aurelius. Mr. Arnold, if I may
say so, carried too far his belief, sound enough so far
as it goes, in the superiority of French prose to French

verse. It is perhaps impossible for an Englishman to appreciate French Alexandrines, unless, like Gibbon, he be half a Frenchman himself. But it is rash for a foreigner to say that the metre of Racine is inadequate, and the verse of the *Phèdre* not a vehicle for "high poetry." And what of this couplet from Victor Hugo ?

> " Et la Seine fuyait avec un triste bruit,
>   Sous ce grand chevalier du gouffre et de la nuit."

Mr. Arnold disliked Alexandrines as he disliked the "heroic" couplets of Pope. But then, these personal distastes are, as he has himself taught us, eccentricities, which criticism rejects as irrelevant. That "Addison has in his prose an intrinsically better vehicle for his genius than Pope in his couplet" is not a self-evident proposition. It must be proved, and Mr. Arnold makes no attempt to prove it. "Pope, in his *Essay on Man*," says Mr. Arnold, is "thus at a disadvantage compared with Lucretius in his poem on Nature: Lucretius has an adequate vehicle, Pope has not. Nay, though Pope's genius for didactic poetry was not less than that of Horace, while his satirical power was certainly greater, still one's taste receives, I cannot but think, a certain satisfaction when one reads the *Epistles* and *Satires* of Horace, which it fails to receive when one reads the *Satires and Epistles* of Pope." Surely this is paradoxical, if not perverse. That Lucretius was a far greater poet than Pope few would, I suppose, deny, and his best hexameters are hardly equalled even by Virgil's. But few and far between are the poetical lines, such as

> " Græcia barbariæ lento collisa duello "

in the *Satires* and *Epistles* of Horace. Horace wrote them in a professedly prose style (*pedestris sermo*) not in poetic form, and to an ordinary ear his numbers (I am not, of course, referring to the Odes) are far less tuneful than Pope's. Strange, too, almost grotesque, is the judgment that Shelley had neither intellectual force enough, nor culture enough, to master the use of words. Was it not this Shelley who wrote the "Adonais," and the "Ode to the West Wind"? The comparison of Mademoiselle de Guérin with Miss Emma Tatham is rather below Mr. Arnold. Poor Miss Tatham and her "union in church-fellowship with the worshippers at Hawley Square Chapel, Margate," might have been allowed to rest in peace. It is never worth while to sneer at other people's religion, even for the pleasure of contrasting Margate with Languedoc.

The essay on Heine, from which I have already quoted the famous passage about the Philistines, contains also a definition of poetry as "the most beautiful, impressive, and widely effective mode of saying things." Perhaps this is a description rather than a definition, and perhaps, on Mr. Arnold's own showing, it would not apply to the French language. But as a general truth it is striking, and it is justified by the experience of mankind. In this same essay, however, he broaches almost, if not quite, for the first time his theory of class, which led him altogether astray. Caste is a reality. Class is a fiction. To make classes real it would be necessary to prohibit intermarriage, or rather it would have been necessary to do so centuries ago. Even then there would still be, as Sam Slick says, a great deal of human nature in people. "Aristocracies," Mr. Arnold tells us, "are, as such, naturally impenetrable by ideas; but their individual members have high courage and a turn for breaking bounds; and a man of genius, who is the born child of the idea, happening to be born in the aristocratic ranks, chafes against the obstacles which prevent him from fully developing it." All this is very fanciful. Byron and Shelley were "members of the aristocratic class." What then? They were Byron and Shelley. They were as unlike each other as two contemporary Englishmen could well be. Byron was childishly and vulgarly proud of his social position. Shelley cared no more for it than he cared for the binomial theorem. The Scottish peasantry are not naturally impenetrable to ideas. But Burns chafed against the obstacles which prevented him from fully developing his genius, and if, as somebody said, Byron was a Harrow boy, Burns was a plough boy. The percentage of impenetrability to ideas is probably much the same in one class as in another. Mr. Arnold pronounces Heine's weakness to have been, not as Goethe said, deficiency in love, but "deficiency in self-respect, in true dignity of character." But this is not literary criticism, and to Heine's literary greatness no man has paid more sympathetic homage than Matthew Arnold.

The essay on "Pagan and Mediæval Religious Sentiment" is best known by the charming translation from the fifteenth Idyll of Theocritus which it contains. But the essay has other, and perhaps higher, merits than this. Gorgo and Praxinoe are indeed delightfully natural characters. The Hymn to Adonis is a beautiful and highly finished piece of composition.

But Theocritus was pre-eminently the poet of passion and of nature. This satirical sketch of town life is one of the least Theocritean things in him. It is, however, admirably suited to Mr. Arnold's purpose, which was to contrast Paganism with Mediævalism, Theocritus with St. Francis. Side by side with the Hymn to Adonis he sets the Canticle of St. Francis, and thus he comments upon them.

"Now, the poetry of Theocritus's hymn is poetry treating the world according to the demand of the senses; the poetry of St. Francis's hymn is poetry treating the world according to the demand of the heart and imagination. The first takes the world by its outward, sensible side; the second by its inward, symbolical side. The first admits as much of the world as is pleasure-giving; the second admits the whole world, rough and smooth, painful and pleasure-giving, all alike, but all transfigured by the power of a spiritual emotion, all brought under a law of supersensual love, having its seat in the soul."

That is Matthew Arnold, as it seems to me, at his very best. Admirable also is this: — "I wish to decide nothing as of my own authority; the great art of criticism is to get oneself out of the way and to let humanity decide." But at the close of the essay he strikes a lower note, he almost touches slang. After a fine translation of a noble passage in Sophocles, he says, "Let St. Francis — nay, or Luther either — beat that!" This is not a dignified finale to a classical piece.

The essay on Joubert is one of Mr. Arnold's most charming and most characteristic studies. Joubert is not, perhaps — indeed Mr. Arnold admits it — a great writer. But he is a most subtle and suggestive one. He is also one whom few English readers would have found out for themselves, and is therefore very well suited for the sort of essay in which Matthew Arnold shone. The comparison with Coleridge, through striking and brilliant, is not very fruitful, for it is rather a contrast than a parallel. The translations from Joubert's *Thoughts*, exquisitely felicitous as they are, seem to me too paraphrastic, too far from the original. The rich excellence of this essay lies in its description of Joubert's character, and of the intellectual atmosphere in which he lived. There is a good deal in Joubert, whose life covered the second half of the eighteenth century, more like Newman than Coleridge. This, for instance : "Do not bring into the domain of reasoning that which belongs to our innermost feeling. State truths of sentiment, and do not try to prove them. There is a danger in such proofs, for in arguing it is necessary to treat that which is in question as something problematic : now that which we accustom ourselves to treat as problematic, ends by appearing to us as really doubtful. . . . 'Fear God' has made many men pious ; the proofs of the existence of God have made many men atheists." There is a passage in the *Grammar of Assent* which may well have been suggested by that. Joubert is not, and never could be, a popular author, and much of his peculiar aroma cannot be preserved in translation. But of religious sentiment, as distinguished from theological dogma, there have been few such fascinating teachers, and this no doubt it was, not merely the praise of Sainte-Beuve, which recommended him to Matthew Arnold. Those who deny the possibility of undogmatic Christianity must, among other things, explain Joubert away.

The two strictly philosophical essays are devoted respectively to Spinoza and to Marcus Aurelius. For the essay on Joubert is more than half literary, while the others are literature pure and simple. Of Matthew Arnold as a philosopher it may be said that, though clear, he was not deep, and that though gentle, he was not dull. He abhorred pedantry so much that he shrank from system, but he always had a keen insight into his author's meaning, and he was a master of lucid exposition. His account of Baruch, or Benedict, Spinoza, cast out of the Portuguese synagogue at Amsterdam with a curse that Ernulphus might have envied, is singularly attractive, as indeed is the man himself. Expelled by the Jews, Spinoza never became a Christian. But in his life he was faultless, and no man better fulfilled the injunction of the prophet Micah, "Do justice and love mercy, and walk humbly with thy God." Although he laboured, like so many profoundly religious men, under the imputation of atheism, he was really, as Goethe said of him, "Gott-betrunken," intoxicated with the divine nature, which he felt around him as well as above him. The Bible, that is to say the Old Testament, was his favourite book, and the subject of his constant study. He was the first and greatest of Biblical critics in the free, modern sense of the term. Being, of course, a Hebrew scholar, and thoroughly acquainted with Oriental modes of expression, he readily perceived, even in the seventeenth century, that many scriptural stories which popular theology even now regards as miraculous were not so intended by those who wrote them. Mr. Arnold does not deal with Spinoza's ethics. They go deeper than he cared to penetrate. But he gives an excellent summary of the *Tractatus Theologico-Politicus*, a treatise on Church and State. That grand old text, "Where the spirit of the Lord is, there is liberty," illustrates at once the politics and the theology of Spinoza. When Mr. Arnold wrote, the only English translation of Spinoza, who composed in Latin, was almost incredibly bad. There is now a remarkably good one by the late Mr. Robert Elwes of Corpus Christi College, Oxford.

Of Marcus Aurelius Mr. Arnold was a devotee. And indeed there are few nobler figures in history than this humble and pious man who, placed at the head of the Roman Empire when the Roman Empire was co-extensive with the civilised world, wrote his imperishable maxims of morality in the intervals of his Dacian campaigns. It is true that he persecuted the Christians. Polycarp of Smyrna suffered under him. But, as Mr. Arnold says, he did it in ignorance. He died in 180, and never saw the Sermon on the Mount, or the Gospel of St. John. In his *Meditations* he never speaks of the Christians at all. He knew nothing about the teaching of Christ, which would have interested him so profoundly. Like Tacitus a century earlier, he regarded the Christians as an obscure sect of the Jews, morose fanatics, despisers of law and reason, enemies of the human race. Constantine in the next century discovered the truth, and became a Christian. But Marcus Aurelius was an infinitely better man than Constantine. In him we have Pagan morality at the highest point it ever attained, as in Petronius we have it at the lowest. No comparison between Christianity and Paganism can be fair which rejects either one of these pictures or the other. The world, said Plato, would never be perfect until kings became philosophers, or philosophers became kings. The world is not likely ever to be perfect. But Marcus was a true philosopher on a throne. He was a real Stoic, yet with something strangely like Christian humility, which the Stoics altogether lacked. He " remains," says Mr. Arnold, " the especial friend and comforter of all clear-headed and scrupulous, yet pure-hearted and upward-striving men, in those ages most especially that walk by sight, not by faith, and yet have no open vision: he cannot give such souls, perhaps, all they yearn for, but he gives them much; and what he gives them they can receive." The Greek of Marcus Aurelius is hard and crabbed — the Greek of a Roman. Even scholars will be glad to read him in the accurate, if not very elegant, version of Mr. Long. He owed much, perhaps more than Mr. Arnold allows, to Epictetus, and he gratefully acknowledges his debt. Epictetus was a slave. At the opposite ends of the long ladder which made up Roman civilisation before Christianity became the faith of the Roman Empire, these two great men are inseparably connected by affinity of soul. " The idea of a polity," wrote the Emperor, " in which there is the same law for all, a polity administered with regard to equal rights and equal freedom of speech, and the idea of a kingly government which respects most of all the freedom of the governed." This ideal was very imperfectly realised in the Roman State. But is it perfectly realised now ?

CHAPTER VII

MR. ARNOLD held the Professorship of Poetry at Oxford for ten years, from 1857 to 1867. He was twice elected for periods of five years each. But for him, as for the President of the United States, a third term was impossible. In 1867 he retired, and was succeeded by Sir Francis Doyle, author of that noble poem "The Return of the Guards," that justly popular poem "The Private of the Buffs," and "The Doncaster St. Leger," the best description of a horse-race ever written in English verse. There were parts of Mr. Arnold's professorial duties, such as reading the Creweian Oration and examining for the Newdigate, which he heartily disliked. But, on the whole, the position gave him great pleasure, and he laid it down with sincere regret. He was anxious that Mr. Browning should succeed him. Mr. Browning, however, was not an Oxford man, and though an honorary Master's Degree had been conferred upon him, the objection was held to be fatal.

The Chair of Poetry is not an exhausting burden, and all the time he held it Mr. Arnold was zealously fulfilling his duty to the Department of Education. In 1865 he undertook another of those Continental investigations which he so thoroughly enjoyed. The Schools Inquiry Commissioners charged him with the

agreeable task — agreeable at least to him — of report-
ing upon the system of teaching for the upper and
middle classes which prevailed in France, Italy,
Germany, and Switzerland. At the beginning of
April he left London for Paris, where he began his
work. In Paris he met a citizen of the United States
who might almost have walked out of *Martin Chuzzlewit.*
Such are scarcely to be found now. "I have just
seen," he writes to his mother on the 1st of May, "an
American, a great admirer of mine, who says that the
three people he wanted to see in Europe were James
Martineau, Herbert Spencer, and myself. His talk
was not as our talk, but he was a good man." The
last touch is characteristically and ironically urbane.
At this time, seven years after "Merope," appeared
"Atalanta in Calydon," which proved as popular as
"Merope" was the reverse. It did not, however,
satisfy Mr. Arnold, and in a critical letter to Professor
Conington, dated the 17th of May, he thus speaks of
it : — "The moderns will only have the antique on the
condition of making it more *beautiful* (according to
their own notions of beauty) than the antique — *i.e.*
something wholly different." This is just criticism
so far as it goes. "Atalanta" is not Greek. It is far
too violent and impulsive to be Greek. But its magnificent verses, with their rush and ring, their surge
and flow, will always raise the spirits and charm the
ear. Conington, a profoundly learned man, but a
pedant if ever there was one, was also, it seems, a
great admirer of "Merope." He must have taken it
with him to the grave, for it died long before its author.
Mr. Arnold did not enjoy Italy so much as he might
have done if he had known more about architecture

and painting. But he was a keen critic of national character, and being at Florence just after Florence had become, for a short time, the capital of Italy, he saw in a moment the weak point of the modern Italians. "They imitate the French too much," he wrote to his mother on the 24th of May. "It is good for us to attend to the French, they are so unlike us, but not good for the Italians, who are a sister nation." Luminous ideas of this kind light up the not very brilliant atmosphere of Mr. Arnold's correspondence, most of which he dashed off at odd moments, without having any special turn for the art. We could well have spared his comparison between the sham, gim-crack cathedral at Milan, which contains half a dozen more beautiful churches, and the great Duomo at Florence, with the cupola of Brunelleschi, unequalled in the world. But the fascination of Italy overcame Mr. Arnold at last, for on the 12th of September he wrote from Dresden to Mr. Slade, that "all time passed in .touring anywhere in Western Europe, except Italy, seemed to him, with his present lights, time misspent," and it does not appear that he ever changed this opinion.

Mr. Arnold was at Zurich in October 1865, when he heard of Lord Palmerston's death. Palmerston, though an aristocrat, as this word is generally under-stood, had none of the cosmopolitan culture which aristocracies are supposed to affect. He was as typical an Englishman as Bright or Cobden, far too typical for Mr. Arnold's taste. But with some allowance for personal prejudice, the following extract from Mr. Arnold's letter to his mother on Palmerston's career has truth as well as point in it. "I do not deny his

popular personal qualities, but as to calling him a
great Minister like Pitt, Walpole, and Peel, and
talking of his death as a national calamity, why,
taking his career from 1830, when his importance
really begins, to the present time, he found his
country the first power in the world's estimation,
and he leaves it the third; of this, no person with
eyes to see and ears to hear, and opportunities for
using them, can doubt; it may even be doubted
whether, thanks to Bismarck's audacity, resolution,
and success, Prussia too, as well as France and the
United States, does not come before England at present in general respect." This contemporary judgment of a calm observer, whose political opinions
were those of an independent Whig, may be com-
mended to believers in the Palmerstonian legend.
Matthew Arnold was the best of sons, and the allusions to his father in his letters to his mother, are
really a more affectionate form of the feeling which
prompted Frederick the Great's filial presents of
gigantic grenadiers. Thus, on the 18th of November
1865, after reading Mr. Stopford Brooke's excellent
Life of Frederick Robertson, he writes: "It is a mistake to put him with papa, as the *Spectator* does:
papa's greatness consists in his bringing such a
torrent of freshness into English religion by placing
history and politics in connection with it; Robertson's
is a mere religous biography, but as a religious biography it is deeply interesting." Mr. Arnold was, of
course, before all things a man of letters, and of physical science he knew little or nothing. It is, therefore,
an interesting proof of his mental width that he should
have strongly recommended to his sister, Mrs. Forster,

science, especially botany, as better suited to cultivate perception in a child than grammar or mathematics. Perhaps he felt the want of scientific training himself. But he was intensely practical, and did his official work far more efficiently than many drudges who never wrote a verse. Just before Lord Russell's Government resigned in 1866, he applied for a Commissionership of Charities. It would, as he told his mother, have given him another three hundred a year, and an independent instead of a subordinate position. No man in England was better qualified for it. His views on charitable endowments were, as almost every one would now admit, thoroughly wise, enlightened, and sound. But the post was wanted for a lawyer, and lawyers, in this country, are made everything except judges. The appointment was Lord Russell's, and Lord Russell, as we know, was one of Mr. Arnold's earliest admirers. Mr. Gladstone, however, had paramount influence, and it is said that he had already discovered the theological heterodoxy which afterwards became patent to the vulgar eye. It is almost inconceivable nowadays that such an argument should have weighed with a Minister filling a purely secular place. Mr. Arnold's failure was a disaster to the public service, and may almost be called a scandal. He was also unsuccessful in the following year, when he applied for the post of Librarian to the House of Commons. His application was supported by Mr. Disraeli, the leader of the House, and by many other distinguished persons. But Speaker Denison had determined to carry out one of those mysterious rearrangements in which the great functionaries of Parliament delight, and this particular plan involved the elevation of the Sub-Librarian, a thoroughly competent man. In this case Mr. Arnold's success would have been a public misfortune, for it would have withdrawn him from work of the greatest value, and laid him, for all practical purposes, on the shelf.

Mr. Arnold's last lectures as Professor of Poetry were devoted to the study of Celtic Literature. They were four in number, and were successively published after delivery in the *Cornhill Magazine*. In 1867, when Mr. Arnold retired from the Chair, they were reprinted in a small volume. Mr. George Smith, the great publisher, remarked that it was not exactly the sort of book which Paterfamilias would buy at a bookstall, and take down to his Jemima. I should be sorry to suggest that Mr. Smith did not get further than the title, to which his remark would apply. But no title was ever more misleading, and few books are easier to read. This is perhaps the most brilliantly audacious of all Mr. Arnold's performances. Mr. Gladstone wrote a book on the Bible without knowing a word of Hebrew. Matthew Arnold wrote, not indeed on Celtic literature, but on the study of it, in happy and contented ignorance of Gaelic, Erse, and Cymry. Only men of genius can do these things. Upon the real nature and value of Celtic literature these charming pages throw little, if any, light. The most solid part consists of notes contributed by Lord Strangford, a scientific philologist, and they are comically like a tutor's corrections of his pupil's exercise. Mr. Arnold tells us, with engaging frankness, how the idea of these lectures arose in his mind. He was staying at Llandudno, and got tired of gazing on the sea, especially on the Liverpool steamboats. So he looked

inland, and studied the local traditions. He even
attended an Eisteddfod, which he describes without
enthusiasm. This national institution was attacked
at that time by a great English newspaper in language of almost inconceivable brutality, which would
be quite impossible now. Mr. Arnold, a true gentleman in the highest meaning of the term, resented the
insult, and the chief merit of his book is its delicately
sympathetic handling of the Celtic character. Admitting that all Welshmen ought to learn English, he
pleads for the preservation of the Welsh language,
and this led him to the "Science of Origins," on which
French scholars have bestowed so much research. He
reminded the English people that they have a Celtic
as well as a Norman element in them, and that to it
they owed much of what was best in their poetry. His
theory that rhyme is Celtic has been disputed, and certainly mediæval Latin is a more obvious source. The
Celtic genius for style, for "melancholy and natural
magic," is perhaps hardly borne out by the few fragments of translation which Mr. Arnold produces.
But the notion of England as "a vast obscure Cymric
basis with a vast visible Teutonic superstructure" is
fascinating, if unknown and unknowable. Of happy
touches this little volume is full. There we have
Luther and Bunyan, whose connection with Celtic
literature is remote, labelled as "Philistines of genius."
There we have the Celt "always ready to react against
the despotism of fact." Touches of human interest
are not wanting. There is Owen Jones, who slowly
and laboriously amassed a fortune that he might spend
it all in printing and publishing every Welsh manu-
script upon which he could lay his hands. There is

H

Eugene O'Curry, the learned and indefatigable student
of his native Erse, who edited the *Annals of the Four
Masters*. To him enters Thomas Moore, lazily contemplating a *History of Ireland*, and remarks profoundly that these Annals "could not have been
written by fools, or for any foolish purpose." What
the *Annals of the Four Masters*, and the *Myvyrian
Archæology*, and Lady Charlotte Guest's *Mabinogion*,
are actually worth, we know no more when we have
finished the book than we knew when we began it.
But for British prejudice against other nationalities it
is a wholesome antidote. In this, as in so many other
respects, Mr. Arnold was in advance of his age, unless,
indeed, we prefer to say that he led his generation to
a culture less partial and more urbane. The sever-
est censor of sciolism, to which perhaps Mr. Arnold
was not wholly a stranger, may well be appeased by
such a charming phrase as "bellettristic trifler," which
this amateur of Celtic applies to himself.

CHAPTER VIII

THE *NEW POEMS*

THE publication of Mr. Arnold's *New Poems* in 1867, though directly suggested by Mr. Browning, who wished to see "Empedocles on Etna" restored to its original shape, was, as he himself said, a labour of love. He has expressed in familiar lines the opinion that poetry which gave no pleasure to the writer will give no pleasure to the world. This volume had an immediate and a permanent success. It bore for motto, besides the sentiment to which reference has already been made, the pretty quatrain, which age cannot wither—

> "Though the Muse be gone away,
> Though she move not earth to-day,
> Souls, erewhile who caught her word,
> Ah! still harp on what they heard."

With these poems the poetical career of Matthew Arnold may be said to close. To the end of his life he wrote occasional verses. But they were few in number, and they neither, with the exception of "Westminster Abbey," added to his fame nor detracted from it. His outward circumstances harmonised with this inward change. Mr. Arnold ceased to be Professor of Poetry. He remained an Inspector of Schools. But his poetical fame was established, and no living English poet except Tennyson was incon-

2768

testably his superior. The greatest poem in the
volume, some think the greatest he ever wrote, is
"Thyrsis," a monody, or elegy, on his friend Arthur
Clough, who had died, as we have seen, at Florence in
1861. Mr. Swinburne, a warm admirer of Matthew
Arnold, has expressed a too contemptuous estimate of
Clough's poetical powers. His English hexameters and
pentameters are doggerel, though the ideas which they
express are often subtle. But some of his shorter pieces,
such as " Say not the struggle nought availeth," and
" As ships at eve becalmed they lay," have retained their
hold upon the minds and hearts of men. Clough is not
likely ever to become a mere name, like the Reverend
Mr. King. That "Thyrsis" is inferior to "Lycidas"
hardly requires stating. All English dirges, except
the dirge in " Cymbeline," are. But in truth the
comparison is fruitless, for there is no resemblance.
Mr. Arnold's model was not Milton, but Theocritus,
and " Thyrsis " is thoroughly Theocritean in sentiment.
The opening stanza strikes the keynote, and is, I
think, unsurpassed throughout the poem. It is
penetrated, like most of the stanzas which succeed it,
with the spirit of the place, and is redolent of the
beautiful country round Oxford —

> " How changed is here each spot man makes or fills !
>   In the two Hinkseys nothing keeps the same ;
>   The village street its haunted mansion lacks,
>   And from the sign is gone Sibylla's name,
>   And from the roof the twisted chimney-stacks ; —
>   Are ye too changed, ye hills ?
>   See, 'tis no foot of unfamiliar men
>   To-night from Oxford up your pathway strays !
>   Here came I often, often, in old days,
>   Thyrsis and I ; we still had Thyrsis then."

" Thyrsis " is avowedly a sequel to " The Scholar Gipsy," with which it should always be read. I do not feel able to decide between their relative merits. Even Oxford has inspired no nobler verse.

But though " Thyrsis " was the principal of the *New Poems,* and the best example of Mr. Arnold's matured powers, there are many others at once excellent and characteristic. " Saint Brandan " is a picturesque embodiment of a strange mediæval legend touching Judas Iscariot, who is supposed to be released from Hell for a few hours every Christmas because he had done in his life a single act of charity. " Calais Sands " and " Dover Beach " strike a higher note. " Calais Sands " is cold compared with the love-poems in " Switzerland." But it is graceful, and charming, and everything except real. " Dover Beach " is very different, and much deeper. Profoundly melancholy in tone, it expresses the peculiar turn of Mr. Arnold's mind, at once religious and sceptical, philosophical and emotional, better than his formal treatises on philosophy and religion. The second part of it deserves to be quoted at length, both on this account and for its literary beauty —

> " The Sea of Faith
> Was once, too, at the full, and round earth's shore
> Lay like the folds of a bright girdle furl'd ;
> But now I only hear
> Its melancholy, long, withdrawing roar,
> Retreating to the breath
> Of the night-wind down the vast edges drear
> And naked shingles of the world.
>
> " Ah, love, let us be true
> To one another ! for the world, which seems

> To lie before us like a land of dreams,
> So various, so beautiful, so new,
> Hath really neither joy, nor love, nor light,
> Nor certitude, nor peace, nor help for pain ;
> And we are here as on a darkling plain
> Swept with confused alarm of struggle and fight,
> Where ignorant armies clash by night ! "

"The Last Word" describes the plight of a hopeless and exhausted struggler against a Philistine world too strong for him. It is one of Mr. Arnold's best known poems, and need not be reprinted here. The last stanza contains a curious, and rather awkward, ambiguity. Thus it runs:—

> "Charge once more, then, and be dumb !
> Let the victors, when they come,
> When the forts of folly fall,
> Find thy body by the wall."

The natural meaning of these words would be that the person addressed had been engaged in defending the forts of folly, which, it need hardly be said, is the precise opposite of what Mr. Arnold intended. "Bacchanalia, or The New Age," is perhaps the most fanciful among all Matthew Arnold's poems, and it is certainly one of the most beautiful. It must be read as a whole, for it illustrates the connection of the past with the present in the mind of a poet. But the following lines would be missed from any estimate or criticism of Matthew Arnold. The constant repetition of a single epithet shows where Mr. Arnold's danger lay, both in prose and verse. In this case, however, the arrangement is so skilful that the trick, for it must be called a trick, justifies itself—

"The epoch ends, the world is still.
The age has talk'd and work'd its fill —
The famous orators have shone,
The famous poets sung and gone.
The famous men of war have fought,
The famous speculators thought,
The famous players, sculptors wrought,
The famous painters fill'd their wall,
The famous critics judg'd it all.
The combatants are parted now,
Unhung the spear, unbent the bow,
The puissant crown'd, the weak laid low ! "

"Rugby Chapel," written so far back as 1857, and
"Heine's Grave," are Mr. Arnold's most successful
efforts in lyrical metre without rhyme. That defect is
to my mind, or rather to my ear, a fatal one. But if
ever Mr. Arnold for a time appears to surmount it, these
are the poems where his apparent success is achieved.
In "Rugby Chapel" he praises his father as one of
those who were not content with saving their own
souls, but sought to bring others with them —

"Then, in such hour of need
Of your fainting, dispirited race,
Ye, like angels, appear,
Radiant with ardour divine.
Beacons of hope, ye appear !
Languor is not in your heart,
Weakness is not in your word,
Weariness not on your brow."

"Heine's Grave" is a painfully morbid poem on a
supremely dismal subject. It contains some grotesque
instances of metrical eccentricity. Such a line as

" Paris drawing-rooms and lamps "

is beyond all criticism, out of the pale. But the famous description of England, or the British Empire, is as good as anything of the kind can be : —

> " Yes, we arraign her ! but she,
>   The weary Titan ! with deaf
>   Ears, and labour-dimm'd eyes,
>   Regarding neither to right,
>   Nor left, goes passively by,
>   Staggering on to her goal ;
>   Bearing on shoulders immense,
>   Atlantean, the load,
>   Well-nigh not to be borne,
>   Of the too vast orb of her fate."

If the thing is to be done at all, that is how one should do it.

The " Stanzas from the Grande Chartreuse," though included in this volume, appeared in *Fraser's Magazine* for April 1855. They are very stately and solemn stanzas. Every one knows the famous lines about Byron, and the " pageant of his bleeding heart." Less familiar, but I think finer, is the author's own attitude of wistful yearning reverence for the comfort of a creed he cannot hold —

> " Wandering between two worlds, one dead,
>   The other powerless to be born,
>   With nowhere yet to rest my head,
>   Like these, on earth I wait forlorn.
>   Their faith, my tears, the world deride —
>   I come to shed them at your side.
>   Oh, hide me in your gloom profound,
>   Ye solemn seats of holy pain !
>   Take me, cowl'd forms, and fence me round,
>   Till I possess my soul again ;

> Till free my thoughts before me roll,
> Not chafed by hourly false control ! "

With these pathetic lines we may take our leave for the present of Mr. Arnold as a poet. He had other work to do, and from duty he never shrank. From this time forth the poetic stream ran thin, though it never quite ran out.

CHAPTER IX

EDUCATION

EDUCATION is proverbially a dull subject. But in Mr. Arnold's case it cannot be omitted, and in his hands it was never dull. He was an Inspector of Schools for five-and-thirty years, resigning his post only two years before his death. The Department wisely and properly treated him with great indulgence. He always had the most interesting work that there was to do. But his life was a laborious one. He was more than willing to spend and be spent for the intellectual improvement of his countrymen. When he was first appointed an Inspector there existed a sort of agreement between Church and State. The Catholic schools were inspected by Catholics; schools belonging to the Church of England were officially visited by clergymen. Being neither a clergyman nor a Catholic, Mr. Arnold was assigned to Protestant schools not connected with the Church of England, or, in other words, to the schools of the Dissenters. He did not get on with Dissenters, and his irritation, as we shall see, found vent in his writings. After 1870, when compulsory education began, and denominational inspection was abandoned, Mr. Arnold confined himself to the borough of Westminster, where for a long time there was only one Board school. He was the idol of

the children, for he petted them and treated them with
the easy condescension which was his charm.   Upon the
teachers his influence was still more important.   "In-
directly," says Sir Joshua Fitch, "his fine taste, his
gracious and kindly manner, his honest and gen-
erous recognition of any new form of excellence
which he observed, all tended to raise the aims and
the tone of the teachers with whom he came in contact,
and to encourage in them self-respect, and respect for
their work."   His official reports were most interesting and instructive.   He had a natural insight into
the real merits and defects of public teaching.   He
saw things as they were.   "The typical mental defect
of our school children," he said, "is their almost
incredible scantiness of vocabulary."   This is a national
deficiency; and no one who has sat, for howsoever
short a time, in Parliament, can believe that it is
peculiar to children.   Mr. Arnold held no narrow or
rigid view of the difference between primary and
secondary education.   He thought that the rudiments of French and Latin might well be taught in
elementary schools.   He was also an advocate for
teaching in them the beginnings of natural science, or
what Huxley used to call "Physiography."   "The
excuse," as he put it characteristically, "for putting
most of these matters into our programme is that
we are all coming to be agreed that an entire ignorance of the system of nature is as grave a defect in
our children's education as not to know that there
ever was such a person as Charles the First."

In 1868 appeared Mr. Arnold's Report upon Schools
and Universities on the Continent.   It deals with education in France, Italy, Germany, and Switzerland.

But its practical interest is restricted to France and
Germany.   For the Swiss system was almost identical
with the German, and in Italy at that time national
education was in its infancy.

French institutions and French habits of thought
were always thoroughly congenial to Mr. Arnold. His
lucid, methodical mind was attracted by the thorough-
ness of French logic, and he was more especially
fascinated by the orderly sequence with which the
pupil ascended from the primary school to the university.   Himself the product of reformed Rugby, and
of unreformed Oxford, a child of the old learning and
the new spirit, he was appalled by the anomalous condition of English universities, and by the chaos of
intermediate teaching in England. With the admirable schools of Scotland he had nothing to do. The
secondary schools of France, all under the Minister
of Education, he described with hearty though not
uncritical praise. The University of Paris, the great
seat of learning in the Middle Ages, moved him to
unwonted enthusiasm. He envied the Professors who
were only teachers, and declared that he would rather
have their moderate salary with abundant leisure than
be a Master in one of our public schools, receiving
twice their pay, but having no time to himself. The
École Normale, the training college for French teachers, he pronounced to be excellent. No one in England was taught to teach, whereas in France the State
made itself directly responsible for all kinds of education, and the most stringent tests were applied to
teachers. Then, again, the French language in France,
unlike the English language in England, was made
the subject of thorough and serious study. Even in

learning the classics the development of the mother
tongue, and its resources, was the first consideration
impressed upon the mind. Examinations, Mr. Arnold
held, were better understood in France than here.
The French did not attempt to examine boys before
they were fifteen, and he held very strongly the
opinion that before that age intellectual pressure
was dangerous.   Between fifteen and twenty-five he
thought that the mind could hardly be overworked.
Tested by results, he showed that the French schools
were far more successful than our own. When he
wrote, there were in the public schools of England
fifteen thousand boys.   In the public schools of
France there were sixty-six thousand. It may, however be doubted whether the standard of comparison
was a fair one. The French lyceums provided for a
class which in England was even more content than it
is now with private or " adventure " schools.

On one point, and that certainly not the least important, Mr. Arnold had to confess that French boarding-
schools were most unsatisfactory. He gave the worst
possible account of the ushers, the *maîtres d'études*.
They were drudges, they were not required to teach,
and they were miserably underpaid.   Their duty was
to protect the morals of the boys, but many of them
were gravely suspected of doing exactly the opposite.
No scientific perfection of teaching can make up for
such an evil as this.   After all, there is something to
be said for the freedom and honour of Eton and Harrow, of Rugby and Winchester. There are cruelty
and vice in all schools.   But constant supervision and
absolute distrust encourage more mischief than they
prevent. In French schools the hours of work are

longer, and the means of recreation scantier, than English boys would endure.

Mr. Arnold's Reports on French, Swiss, and Italian Education were never republished. To his Report on the Education of Germany he must himself have attached more value, for he brought it out again in 1874, and a third time in 1882. Perhaps he considered the example of a Teutonic race more likely to be contagious. The cheapness of German education struck him forcibly, and though prices had nearly doubled before the reappearance of his Report, he maintained that the relative proportion between the two countries was the same. This could not be said now, but there is still much room for economy in the public schools and universities of England. German schools, as Mr. Arnold found them, were denominational, with a conscience clause, and attendance at them was compulsory for all classes. In Prussia, which Mr. Arnold took as typical of Germany, the Government, as in France, set up an educational ladder which a promising boy could mount from the bottom rung to the top. Adepts in education were consulted by the State, as they were not in England. This was a point which Mr. Arnold put very strongly, and he urged it with some exaggeration. It is not quite true that expert opinion has been rejected by the Education Department, now the Board of Education. Mr. Arnold's own Reports, for instance, were very carefully considered by his official superiors, and of Education Commissions there has been no end. The difficulties in carrying out their recommendations have been Parliamentary, and the great difficulty of all has been the religious one. In Germany, as in France, the mother tongue was carefully taught, and in the *Realschule*, intended to prepare boys for business, English was obligatory, as well as French. In England the teaching of foreign languages has made much progress since Mr. Arnold's day, but the study of English is confined to elementary schools. The public, or national, schools of Prussia are not boarding-schools, and the boys are, or were, for the most part taken in by private families. The German universities are the only avenue to the learned professions, and, as is well known, a German professor, though receiving, according to our standard, a small salary, holds a position of great dignity. Admittance to a German university is obtained only by examination, and the test is a severe one. For the teachers there is a very stringent examination indeed. They have to graduate in "pædagogic" before they reach the *facultas docendi*. Mr. Arnold was conscious that to most Englishmen all this would seem mere pedantry. No man was less of a pedant than he. But he held that his countrymen's ideas of education were hopelessly unscientific, and he did his best to correct them. He believed in the State as an instrument of education, as we have all come to believe in it now, and the official position of German universities was congenial to him. At the same time, the German teachers were not, as the French were, liable to dismissal by the Government. Mr. Arnold may fairly be said to have fallen in love with the German system of education. The French universities, he said, wanted liberty; the English universities wanted science; the German universities had both.

In conclusion, Mr. Arnold recommended that Greek and Latin should be studied in England more after the fashion of modern languages. The German boys he found inferior to the English in composition, where English scholarship has always been peculiarly strong. But the making of Latin verses is not, even in this country, so favourite a pursuit as it was fifty or a hundred years ago, and the scientific study of comparative philology has seriously modified classical education. Our secondary schools, to whose badness Mr. Arnold traced an undue distinction between classes in England, are almost as bad as ever. But some of his proposals have been carried out. He was the real father of university extension, and he recommended that the University of London should be made a teaching institution, as it was twelve years after his death. Of all educational reformers in the last century, not excepting his father, Mr. Arnold was the most enlightened, the most far-sighted, and the most fair-minded.

CHAPTER X

MATTHEW ARNOLD always disclaimed the epithet Philosopher, just as he repudiated the title of Professor. But he had a philosophy of his own, which was perhaps, like Cicero's, rather Academic than Stoic or Epicurean. He was always much interested in the history of religion, and he took great delight in Deutsch's famous essay on the Talmud, which appeared in the *Quarterly Review* for October 1867. He wrote about it to Lady de Rothschild on the 4th of November in a letter which well deserves to be quoted, because it contains the germ of a theory that afterwards coloured almost the whole of his writings. What he liked best himself, he said, in the article, were " the long extracts from the Talmud itself," which gave him " huge satisfaction." With the Christian character of later Judaism he was already well acquainted. " It is curious," he added, " that, though Indo-European, the English people is so constituted and trained that there is a thousand times more chance of bringing it to a more philosophical conception of religion than its present conception of Christianity as something utterly unique, isolated, and self-subsistent, through Judaism and its phænomena, than through Hellenism and its phænomena." Mr. Arnold's interest in such matters,

I   113

however, did not take his mind off politics, upon which he always kept a very keen eye. His theory of the Clerkenwell explosion, in December 1867, was at least original. He traced it to the immunity of the Hyde Park rioters in 1866. " You cannot," he wrote to his mother on the 14th of December, "you cannot have one measure for Fenian rioting and another for English rioting, merely because the design of Fenian rioting is more subversive and desperate. What the State has to do is to put down *all* rioting with a strong hand, or it is sure to drift into troubles." It is true, but not the whole truth. Sir Robert Peel once said that everybody told him he ought to be firm, as if he did not know that, and as if the whole art of statesmanship consisted in firmness. The rioters of 1866 might say that they carried the Reform Act of 1867, and the rioters of 1867 might say that they disestablished the Irish Church in 1869. But, as a matter of fact, the rioters of 1867 were dangerous, and the rioters of 1866 were not.

In the same letter, Mr. Arnold mentions a tribute from a teacher of which he felt justly proud. He " was always gentle and patient with the children." No inspector of schools has ever been more universally beloved, though some, it must be confessed, have taken their duties in a more serious spirit. At the beginning of 1868 he was amused and pleased at an invitation from the proprietors of the *Daily Telegraph* to write them a notice of Blake the artist, and to "name his own price." " I sent a civil refusal," he characteristically remarks; " but, you may depend upon it, Lord Lytton was right in saying that it is no inconsiderable advantage to you that all the writing world have a kind of weakness for you even at the time they are attacking you." Early this year, Mr. Arnold moved from London to Harrow for the better education of his children. At Harrow, on the 23rd of November, his eldest son, who had always been an invalid, died, and on the next day Mr. George Russell found the father seeking consolation from the pages of his favourite Marcus Aurelius. His feeling for religion was never confined to Christianity.

Early in 1867 Messrs. Smith and Elder — that is to say, Mr. Arnold's valued friend of a lifetime, Mr. George Smith — published *Culture and Anarchy*, which contains the writer's philosophical system, so far as he had one. Systematic thought he half ironically disclaimed. But he meant even by the title of his book to convey that lawlessness was the result of not deferring to the authority of cultivated persons. There was point in the sarcasm of the Nonconformist critic who spoke of Mr. Arnold's belief in the well-known preference of the Almighty for University men. It is, however, undeniably true that whereas in France and Germany people have too little regard for individual freedom, in England adepts are slighted, knowledge undervalued, and the claim of every man to do as he pleases elevated from a legal doctrine into a moral ideal. There is some truth, though also some exaggeration, in the following passage : " While on the Continent the idea prevails that it is the business of the heads and representatives of the nation, by virtue of their superior means, power, and information, to set an example and to provide suggestions of right reason, among us the idea is that the business of the heads and representatives of the nation is to do nothing of the kind, but applaud the natural taste for the bathos showing itself vigorously in any part of the community, and to encourage its works" (*Culture and Anarchy*, second edition, p. 115). That is what Mr. Arnold would himself have called a heightened and telling way of putting it. But he was attacking a real error, of which practical politics afford numerous examples. It is difficult to be personal without being offensive. If I could avoid offence by taking two instances from the same party, I should say that Mr. Chamberlain represented the theory assailed by Mr. Arnold (for which there is much to be said), and Mr. Balfour the theory he would have substituted for it.

Culture, says Mr. Arnold in his Preface (page x.), is "a pursuit of our total perfection by means of getting to know, on all the matters which most concern us, the best which has been thought and said in the world." In this respect no man ever practised what he preached more thoroughly than Matthew Arnold. To use a phrase widely current of late, he was "the fine flower of Oxford culture," and there has seldom been a more delicate, or a more delightful specimen. Yet he belonged, as he often said, to the middle class, whom he called Philistines, implying that culture was what they lacked. Philistinism is a convenient and expressive term. But it describes a frame of mind, not a class. Mr. Arnold, as I have said before, used the word "class" as if it were synonymous with caste, which in English society does not exist. Common occupations, common professions, above all, intermarriage, make it impossible. There is nothing, except his title, to distinguish a lord from a commoner. The richest people are not the best educated, nor the worst. Mr. Arnold called "the aristocracy," which he would have been puzzled to define, barbarians, because they cared more for field sports than for the improvement of their minds. Some of them do, some of them do not. There is no rule. The love of sport pervades the working classes as well as the House of Lords. Mr. Arnold's name for the proletariate was a confession of failure. He simply called them " the populace," which is no more descriptive than Mr. Bright's "residuum." The English people do not live in classes, they live as individuals, and in sets. Culture and ignorance, simplicity and vulgarity, high and low ideals, are pretty equally divided among all sections of the community. Mr. Arnold refers (at page xviii. of his Preface) to the "undesirable provincialism of the English Puritans and Protestant Nonconformists." If by provincialism (a rather "provincial" word) is meant narrowness of view, it might apply to the school of Mr. Spurgeon, but it certainly would not apply to the school of Dr. Martineau. It would be as reasonable to lump Dr. Creighton with Dr. Ryle because both were Anglican Bishops.

In *Culture and Anarchy*, Mr. Arnold preaches his favourite doctrine of " sweetness and light." The phrase, as he acknowledged, is Swift's. Swift used it of the bees, because they make honey and wax. Mr. Arnold transferred it to the operation of culture, which would, if it could, "make reason and the will of God prevail." He contrasted it with the motto of the *Nonconformist* newspaper : " The Dissidence of Dissent and the Protestantism of the Protestant religion." It is easy to be sarcastic upon this pugnacious device, and to quote St. Peter's " Be of one mind "; but without Protestantism, which is a form of Dissent,

Mr. Arnold's books would have been condemned and suppressed. The religious freedom in which he so lavishly indulged, was secured for him by the objects of his constant gibes. Mr. Arnold's official connection with Oxford had now ceased, but her hold upon his allegiance was undiminished. " We have not won our political battles," he says, at page 32, " we have not carried our main points, we have not stopped our adversaries' advance, we have not marched victoriously with the modern world; but we have told silently upon the mind of the country, we have prepared currents of feeling which sap our adversaries' position when it seems gained, we have kept up our own communications with the future." Who are "we"? Mr. Arnold means Oxford men, and he refers to the Oxford Movement. But Oxford would have condemned Newman's most famous Tract if two High Church proctors had not interfered, and the same Oxford actually degraded Dr. Ward for writing a High Church book. The intellectual, as distinguished from the political, Liberalism of Oxford dates from the admission of Nonconformists. It is only fair to add, before leaving this part of the subject, that Mr. Arnold himself acknowledges his tripartite division of society not to be mutually exclusive. " An English barbarian who examines himself," he says, on page 96, " will in general find himself to be not so entirely a barbarian, but that he has in him also something of the Philistine, and even something of the Populace as well. And the same with Englishmen of the other two classes." Just so. But, then, what is the value of the classification? One is reminded of Thurlow's famous remark about Kenyon and Buller. A rule with too many exceptions ceases to be a rule at all.

"No man," says Mr. Arnold, at page 163, "no man
who knows nothing else knows even his Bible." The
sentiment is familiar; and Mr. Rudyard Kipling has
performed a variation upon it in his celebrated, but
fallacious, inquiry, "What can they know of England
who only England know?" The answer to Mr. Kipling
is — "Everything, if they read the newspapers." Mr.
Arnold was aiming at Mr. Spurgeon, but he hit Bunyan
without meaning it. If stupid people would read the
Bible less, and clever people would read it more, the
world would be much improved. The objects of Mr.
Arnold's just scorn were not really men who confined
themselves to the Bible, but those who tried to serve
God and Mammon. Such, for example, was a late
Chairman of the Great Western Railway, who quoted
to the workmen at Swindon the beautiful sentence
uttered to him every morning by his mother when he
went to work on the line. "Ever remember, my dear
Dan," said the good lady, "that you should look forward to being some day manager of that concern." The
words of the Gospel were fulfilled in Dan. He had
his reward. He did become manager of that not very
well-managed concern. He was outwardly more fortunate than the secretary of the insurance company
who committed suicide because he "laboured under
the apprehension that he would come to poverty, and
that he was eternally lost." Against the vulgar degra-
dation of religion, as unchristian as it is gloomy and
sordid, implied in these awful words, Matthew Arnold set his face, and so far he followed the teaching of Christ.

Mr. Arnold had now a European reputation as a man
of letters, and at the beginning of 1869 the Italian

Government proposed to him that Prince Thomas of Savoy, the Duke of Genoa, who a year afterwards refused the crown of Spain, should live with the Arnolds at Harrow while he attended the school. The proposal would not have been attractive to every one, but it suited Mr. Arnold very well. He was sociable in his tastes, and cosmopolitan in his sympathies. He had travelled a good deal on the Continent, and knew foreign languages well. Mrs. Arnold had no objection, and she, after all, as he remarked to his mother, was the person most concerned. The arrangement answered perfectly, and Mr. Arnold, who loved young people, became very fond of the prince. The boy was a Roman Catholic, but there seems to have been no apprehension that Mr. Arnold would subvert his faith; and when he left Harrow in 1871, his host received from Victor Emmanuel "the Order of Commander of the Crown of Italy." Mr. Arnold's failure in getting a Commissionership under his brother-in-law's Endowed Schools' Act he attributed, no doubt correctly, to Mr. Gladstone; but the disappointment was not very keen, and when the Conservatives came into power five years afterwards, they put a summary end to the Commission. On the other hand, he thoroughly appreciated the honorary degree conferred upon him by his own University at the Commemoration of 1870. The list was made out by the new Chancellor, Lord Salisbury, who had succeeded Lord Derby the year before, and none of the names chosen did more credit to his choice than Mr. Arnold's. He was presented to Lord Salisbury by his friend Mr. Bryce, the Professor of Civil Law, and received by graduates as well as undergraduates with a heartiness which greatly pleased him.

This year 1870 may be assigned as the date of
Matthew Arnold's open breach with the religious, or
at least the orthodox, world. The later stages of that
quarrel, not in all respects creditable to either side,
will be traced in the next chapter, which will be
devoted to Mr. Arnold's theology. *St. Paul and
Protestantism, with an Essay on Puritanism in the
Church of England*, was reprinted, like *Culture and
Anarchy*, from the *Cornhill Magazine*. It is rather
philosophical than theological, and carries a step
further the principles laid down in *Culture and
Anarchy*. Its object was twofold. The author desired to contrast Hebraism, the philosophy of morals,
with Hellenism, the philosophy of thought. He
sought also to prove that Evangelical Puritanism,
which grounded itself upon the doctrines of St. Paul,
had misunderstood and perverted the teaching of the
apostle. Of Evangelical Puritanism the Nonconformists
were the chief representatives, and therefore they come
in for a peculiar share of Mr. Arnold's attention; but
he deals also with the Evangelical party in the Church
of England, then stronger, at least among the clergy,
than it is now. Translating, or paraphrasing, the
Greek word Ἐπιείκεια by "sweet reasonableness," he
urged that that was the distinguishing characteristic
which St. Paul had derived from the teaching of his
Master. Setting this against the spirit of contentious-
ness which, in his opinion, Dissent developed, he
proceeded to argue in favour of unity, of one Church.
So far his position was thoroughly agreeable to the
Anglican Establishment. But it soon appeared that
the new and universal Church was to be purged of all
dogma. God was no longer to be, as the Calvinists

made Him, "a magnified and non-natural man," but
" that stream of tendency by which all things strive to
fulfil the law of their being." This is Pantheism, pure
and simple. Now Pantheism, though a profoundly
religious creed, is not regarded with favour by orthodox
Protestants, or, for that matter, by orthodox Catholics.
I remember that, when I was at Oxford, a Bampton
Lecturer incurred much ridicule by this passionate
adjuration from the pulpit: "I beseech you, brethren,"
said he, "by the mercies of Christ, that you hold fast
to the integrity of your anthropomorphism." It was
enough to make Dean Mansel turn in his grave. But,
as Mr. Goldwin Smith, in a brilliant though now forgotten essay, and Mr. Mill, in his examination of Sir
William Hamilton's Philosophy, reminded Mr. Mansel,
a Deity of whom no human or natural qualities can
be predicated is a mere abstraction, and for practical
purposes might as well not exist.

What, then, according to Mr. Arnold, was St. Paul's
real doctrine? It will be found on page 42 of the
second edition. "This man, whom Calvin and Luther
and their followers have shut up into the two scholas-
tic doctrines of election and justification, would have
said, could we hear him, just what he said about cir-
cumcision and uncircumcision in his own day: 'Election is nothing, and justification is nothing, but the
keeping of the commandments of God.'" It may be
so. What has been said generally of the Bible is true
especially of St. Paul. Everybody goes to the Pauline
Epistles for his own doctrines, and everybody finds
them. They are far more difficult to understand than
Plato or Aristotle, and yet preachers wholly innocent
of hermeneutics will expound them with the most

touching confidence.   Mr. Arnold had a short way of
eliminating from St. Paul what he did not like, such
as "the harsh and unedifying image of the clay and
the potter."   St. Paul "was led into difficulty by the
tendency, which we have already noticed as marking
his real imperfection both as a thinker and as a writer
— the tendency to Judaise" (page 97).   It is hardly
strange that St. Paul should have Judaised.   He was
a Jew, a Pharisee, familiar not merely with the law
and the prophets, but also with the Rabbinical traditions, long before he heard of Christ.   Conversion
changes, or ought to change, a man's purpose and mode
of life.   It does not affect the habits of his mind.   St.
Paul wished to reconcile Christianity with Judaism,
not to supersede one by the other.   His "tendency to
Judaise" is part of his system.   Take it away, and he
ceases to be St. Paul.

In the essay on Puritanism and the Church of
England Mr. Arnold points out (page 129), "that the
High Church divines of the seventeenth century were
Arminian, that the Church of England was the stronghold of Arminianism, and that Arminianism is an
effort of man's practical good sense to get rid of what
is shocking to it in Calvinism."   And he traces the
existence of Nonconformity mainly to the fact that
the Church would not "put the Calvinistic doctrines
more distinctly into her formularies."   This is more
than doubtful history.   The persecuting policy of
Laud, and the Act of Uniformity passed when that
most Christian king, Charles the Second, was restored
to the throne, were the chief causes of Protestant
Dissent.   Mr. Arnold was fond of Butler, and quoted
him almost as often as he quoted the Vulgate.   "'The

Bible,' said the great bishop, ' contains many truths
as yet undiscovered,' and in so saying he passed sentence on every creed and council " (page 151). That
is an admirable application of a profound truth, whether
Butler would himself have made it or not.   For if it
be true, as Cardinal Newman says, that we " cannot
halve the gospel of God's grace," so neither can we
limit it.   *Securus judicat orbis terrarum.*   These words
of St. Augustine convinced Newman that the Church
of Rome must be in the right.   For that purpose Mr.
Arnold, of course, rejects them.   But he adopts them
in support of his own theory that religion implies
unity.   For my part, I think that the words are
much nearer the truth if construed as a classical
Roman would have construed them.   When Horace
wrote that he was " quid Tiridaten terreat unice
securus," he did not mean that he had infallible
knowledge of what frightened Tiridates.   He meant
that he did not care, which is only too true of the
world and theology.   Mr. Arnold defends the Church
of England from the charge of " not knowing her own
mind," or, rather, he denies that it is a charge, and
claims it is as a merit.   He pleads with eloquence and
sincerity that doctrinal differences, however fundamental, are no ground for separation, and that Luther
did not separate for any such reason, but because the
Church of Rome was immoral, which was a true
ground, and the only true one.   This idea of a universal Church, with departure from iniquity for its
first principle, is a very noble one.   The invisible tie
which unites all good men is in some sort a fulfilment
of it.   Fully realised on earth it is never likely to be.
As Mr. Jowett so beautifully says of Plato's *Republic*

the moment we seem to comprehend it, it eludes our
grasp, and at length fades away into the Heavens.
Perhaps Mr. Arnold knew that. There is nothing in
the book to prove that he did not know it.

Mr. Arnold's "genial and somewhat esoteric philosophy," if I may borrow a phrase applied by Sir
George Trevelyan to his uncle, is nowhere more com-
pendiously stated than in *Friendship's Garland*, which
appeared in a complete form at the beginning of 1871.
The history of this little book is curious. The letters
of which it consists were first printed in the *Pall Mall
Gazette*, when that journal of many vicissitudes was
edited by Mr. Frederick Greenwood. They extend
over a period of four years, from 1866 to 1870, dealing
chiefly with the victories of Prussia over Austria, and
of Germany over France. Attributed to a young
Prussian, Arminius von Thunder-ten-Tronckh, whose
name is of course taken from *Candide*, they really
represent Mr. Arnold's views upon the characteristic
deficiencies of his countrymen. It is a remarkable
fact that, though an unsparing critic of English foibles,
and also of the qualities upon which Englishmen
particularly pride themselves, he never became unpopular. Such is the power of urbanity. The outer
public, the widest circle of readers, knew Matthew
Arnold chiefly from quotations in newspapers, and
the readers of the old *Pall Mall* were of the "kid
glove persuasion." But, as he said himself, the writing people had a kindness for him ; and even those at
whom his shafts of ridicule were directed laughed,
unless they were translators of Homer, as heartily as
anybody else. I can myself (and so can Mr. George
Russell) testify to the fact that Mr. Sala, one of Mr.

Arnold's favourite butts, regarded his facetious tor-
mentor with friendly and respectful admiration. This
was very creditable to Mr. Sala, but it was creditable
to Mr. Arnold too. There was plenty of salt in his
wit, and not much pepper. *Friendship's Garland*
is by far the most amusing book he ever wrote, and,
indeed, for anything better of its kind we must go
to Voltaire. Yet nothing would induce Mr. Arnold to
publish a second edition of it, and for many years
before his death it was out of print. He thought it
ephemeral, as parts of it no doubt are, and his fastidious taste condemned it to oblivion. Fortunately, the
destinies of a book are not under the permanent con-
trol of the author, and in 1898 *Friendship's Garland*
was brought out once more. The special phase of
smug, complacent Philistine Liberalism, at which it is
chiefly aimed, had ceased to be predominant. But the
fun is immortal, and the criticism deep as well as
sound. If the book can be said to have a practical
moral, it is that Englishmen should practise the virtue
of obedience, and improve the education of the middle
classes.   But the charm of these pages, the most
vivacious that even Mr. Arnold ever penned, lies in
the inimitable drollness of the social satire, and perhaps I can hardly do better than quote at full length
the conversation between Arminius and the author
upon the justices at petty sessions.

"'The three magistrates in that inn,' said I, 'are not
three Government functionaries all cut out of one block ;
they embody our whole national life ; — the land, religion,
commerce, are all represented by them. Lord Lumpington
is a peer of old family and great estate ; Esau Hittall is a
clergyman ; Mr. Bottles is one of our self-made middle-class

men. Their politics are not all of one colour, and that
colour the Government's. Lumpington is a constitutional
Whig; Hittall is a benighted old Tory. As for Mr. Bottles,
he is a Radical of the purest water; quite one of the Manchester school. He was one of the earliest free-traders, he
has always gone as straight as an arrow about Reform; he
is an ardent voluntary in every possible line, opposed the
Ten Hours' Bill, was one of the leaders of the Dissenting
opposition out of Parliament which smashed up the education clauses of Sir James Graham's Factory Act; and he
paid the whole expenses of a most important church-rate
contest out of his own pocket. And, finally, he looks forward to marrying his deceased wife's sister. Table, as my
friend Mr. Grant Duff says, the whole Liberal creed, and in
not a single point of it will you find Bottles tripping.'
'That is all very well as to their politics,' said Arminius,
'but I want to hear about their education and intelligence.'
'There, too, I can satisfy you,' I answered. 'Lumpington
was at Eton. Hittall was on the foundation at Charterhouse, placed there by his uncle, a distinguished prelate,
who was one of the trustees. You know we English have
no notion of your bureaucratic tyranny of treating the ap-
pointments to these great foundations as public patronage,
and vesting them in a responsible minister; we vest them in
independent magnates, who relieve the State of all work and
responsibility, and never take a shilling of salary for their
trouble. Hittall was the last of six nephews nominated to
the Charterhouse by his uncle, this good prelate, who had
thoroughly learnt the divine lesson that charity begins at
home.' 'But I want to know what his nephew learnt,' interrupted Arminius, 'and what Lord Lumpington learnt at
Eton.' 'They followed,' said I, 'the grand, old, fortifying,
classical curriculum.' 'Did they know anything when they
left?' asked Arminius. 'I have seen some longs and shorts
of Hittall's,' said I, 'about the Calydonian Boar, which were
not bad. But you surely don't need me to tell you, Arminius,
that it is rather in training and bracing the mind for future
acquisition — a course of mental gymnastics we call it — than
in teaching any set thing, that the classical curriculum is so

valuable.' 'Were the minds of Lord Lumpington and Mr. Hittall much braced by their mental gymnastics?' inquired Arminius. 'Well,' I answered, 'during their three years at Oxford they were so much occupied with Bullingdon and hunting, that there was no great opportunity to judge. But for my part I have always thought that their both getting their degree at last with flying colours, after three weeks of a famous coach for fast men, four nights without going to bed, and an incredible consumption of wet towels, strong cigars, and brandy and water, was one of the most astonishing feats of mental gymnastics I ever heard of.' 'That will do for the land and the Church,' said Arminius; 'and now let us hear about commerce.' 'You mean how was Bottles educated?' answered I. 'Here we get into another line altogether, but a very good line in its way, too. Mr. Bottles was brought up at the Lycurgus House Academy, Peckham. You are not to suppose from the name of Lycurgus that any Latin and Greek was taught in the establishment; the name only indicates the moral discipline, and the strenuous earnest character, imparted there. As to the instruction, the thoughtful educator who was principal of the Lycurgus House Academy, — Archimedes Silverpump, Ph.D., you must have heard of him in Germany? — had modern views. "We must be men of our age," he used to say. "Useful knowledge, living languages, and the forming of the mind through observation and experiment, these are the fundamental articles of my educational creed." Or as I have heard his pupil Bottles put it in his expansive moments after dinner: "Original man, Silverpump! fine mind! fine system. None of your antiquated rubbish — all practical work — latest discoveries in science — mind constantly kept excited — lots of interesting experiments — lights of all colours — fizz! fizz! bang! bang! That's what I call forming a man!"' 'And pray,' cried Arminius impatiently, 'what sort of man do you suppose this infernal quack really formed in your precious friend Mr. Bottles?' 'Well,' I replied, 'I hardly know how to answer that question. Bottles has certainly made an immense fortune; but as to Silverpump's effect on his mind, whether it was from any fault in the

Lycurgus House system, whether it was that with a sturdy
self-reliance thoroughly English, Bottles, ever since he quitted
Silverpump, left his mind wholly to itself, his daily newspaper, and the Particular Baptist minister under whom he
sat, or from whatever cause it was, certainly his mind, *quâ*
mind —— ' 'You need not go on,' interrupted Arminius, 'I
know what that man's mind, *quâ* mind, is, well enough.' "

I do not think that Matthew Arnold ever surpassed
this dialogue.   The only criticism I should make upon
it is that the Deceased Wife's Sister Bill got upon his
nerves, and that he always seemed to regard it as a
compulsory measure.   Public opinion, however, was to
some extent with him, for it has not yet become law.

K

CHAPTER XI

IF any formal theologian should cast a roving eye over this book, or over this chapter, he will probably deny that Mr. Arnold had any theology at all. For just as Mr. Frederic Harrison " sought vainly in him a system of philosophy with principles coherent, inter-dependent, subordinate, and derivative," so Mr. Glad-stone observed, with less pedantry, and more humour, that he combined a sincere devotion to the Christian religion with a faculty for presenting it in such a form as to be recognisable neither by friend nor foe. This is a more " damning sentence," to adopt Mr. Arnold's own phrase, than Mr. Harrison's. It is indeed the best and tersest criticism ever passed upon Mr. Arnold's theological writings. I am not in the least inclined to agree with Mr. Russell, who dismisses those writ-ings in a sigh, or with Professor Saintsbury, who dis-poses of them with a sneer. I do not understand how a real scholar like Mr. Saintsbury can think, that unless the Fourth Gospel is " revelation," its date is imma-terial, whether that date were the first century, the fourth century, or the fourteenth. On the contrary, it seems to me that Mr. Arnold set before himself a perfectly legitimate, and even laudable object, but that with many brilliant qualifications there were fatal obstacles to his success. The date of the Gospels,

and the history of their composition, are not merely
interesting in themselves, but absolutely essential to
the estimate of their historical value. Nobody says
that the first Decade of Livy is "revelation." But its
almost total worthlessness as history is mainly, though
not entirely, due to the distance between the age of
Augustus and the age of the kings.

Mr. Arnold's Biblical criticism was not substantially
original. He availed himself of researches made by
more learned men, such as Ewald, Gesenius, and
Kuenen. His treatment of the subject was his own,
and it was not in all respects fortunate. *St. Paul and
Protestantism* is not really a theological book. Writing on the 20th of September 1872 to his friend
M. Fontanès, a French pastor of the broad school, he
says : "En parlant de St. Paul, je n'ai pas parlé en
théologien, mais en homme de lettres mécontent de
la très mauvaise critique littéraire qu'on appliquait
à un grand esprit ; si j'avais parlé en théologien on
ne m'eût pas écouté." The author of *Literature and
Dogma* was certainly heard, and heard with attention,
though not always with approval. Before, however,
dealing with that work, I must mention some pre-
liminary matters. In the same letter from which I
have just quoted, written throughout in French, Mr.
Arnold refers to a little work on Isaiah just published,
which was succeeding "well enough." The success
was not permanent, nor was it of the kind which
Mr. Arnold especially desired. *The Great Prophecy
of Israel's Restoration* was intended for use in elementary schools. Sir Joshua Fitch informs us that
it has never been used in a single school. It has long
been out of print, and is now exceedingly scarce. It

contains the last twenty-seven chapters of Isaiah, with
a long explanatory preface, rather copious notes, and
a few changes in the English of the Authorised Version.   Mr. Arnold's purpose was to help English
school-children in reading these wonderful chapters
"without being frequently stopped by passages of
which the meaning is almost or quite unintelligible."
The little book appeared before the Revised Version
of the Old Testament was finished, but it cannot be
said to have been superseded by that translation, for
one is almost as dead as the other.   The Authorised
Version of the Bible has defects as well as beauties,
among which the reckless and indiscriminate use of
pronouns is perhaps the most prominent.   But it has
a hold upon the English people which nothing can
shake, and Dr. Newman felt its loss more acutely
than anything else when he left the Church of England.   "Who hath believed our report?" may be an
obvious mistranslation.   But there is no more chance
of getting rid of it than of expunging "I know that
my Redeemer liveth" on similar grounds from the
Book of Job.   Still it is a good thing to read these
chapters as a whole, and they have no connection
whatsoever with the rest of Isaiah.

In February 1872 Matthew Arnold's second son
died at Harrow, aged eighteen, and was buried with
his two brothers at Laleham.   The following year he
removed from Harrow, which had too many sad asso-
ciations for Mrs. Arnold, and settled at Pain's Hill,
Cobham, Surrey, which was his home for the remainder
of his life.

The publication of *Literature and Dogma* in 1873
marks a distinct and definite epoch of Matthew

Arnold's life. With this book he severed himself from
orthodox Christianity, and even from Unitarianism
as commonly understood. He had, indeed, a curious
dislike of Unitarians, whom he called Socinians, which
he may have inherited from his father. Yet his own
creed, if creed it can be called, would have horrified
Dr. Arnold far more than theirs. For he rejected not
merely miracles, but the personality of God. Nor, it
must be admitted, did he always express himself in
reverent language, and with a due regard for the feelings of others. He gave intense pain to a distinguished
philanthropist, whose own beliefs were of the straitest,
by comparing him with the Persons of the Trinity, and
though he afterwards withdrew this unseemly jest,
singularly devoid of humour as it was, the bad impression it created remained, because it was the index to
a frame of mind. The reference to "the Bishops of
Winchester and Gloucester" was more pardonable,
because it was founded on a phrase or phrases used
by themselves. But it was in bad taste, and the needless repetition of it is most wearisome. Repetition is
the besetting sin of Mr. Arnold's later prose. It was
ever the fault of our English nation, said the man who
knew the English nation best, that when they have
a good thing they make it too common. Mr. Arnold
happened early in life to stamp one or two happy
expressions upon English literature. He was thereby
encouraged to say a thing over and over again merely
because he thought it particularly good himself. That
is bad literature, and even bad journalism, though it
is, alas, very common. Another tiresome trick which
grew upon Mr. Arnold with advancing years, was the
use of the first person plural for the first person

singular. "We" in a leading article may be defended
because an article sometimes expresses the writer's
opinion as well as the editor's. "We" in a book is
mere affectation, unless there are more authors than
one.

These, however, are superficial criticisms, though
necessary to be made. The book is one of great power
and beauty, saturated with religious sentiment, and
inculcating the loftiest standard of morals. It is, perhaps, an instance of Nemesis that for once Mr. Arnold's
humour fails him. The University of Cambridge provided him with an admirable opportunity by setting
as a subject for a prize poem the words of Lucretius,
Hominum divumque voluptas, alma Venus. But he did
not rise to it. The attempt is a failure. The object of
the book, on the other hand, is wholly serious, and
wholly laudable. It is to free Christianity from excres-
cences which, in Mr. Arnold's opinion, had corrupted
the essence and marred the utility of Christ's teaching.
The quotations on the title-page indicate its scope.
They are from the Vulgate, from Senancour, the
author of *Obermann,* and from Bishop Butler. Butler
argues, in his weighty and dignified manner, that fresh
discoveries may be made in the interpretation of the
Bible, just as they are made in the field of natural
science. Butler was not quite so orthodox as Mr.
Gladstone would have us suppose.

No candid mind could, I think, find any fault with
the aim of Mr. Arnold's theological writings. Goethe
told Eckermann that he thought his books had given
men a new and enlarged sense of freedom. That was
Mr. Arnold's desire, and it is surely a laudable one.
The discussion of his methods is a delicate task. I

know the heat of the fires which are banked beneath those treacherous ashes. Mr. Arnold had become alarmed by the attitude of the working classes towards the Christian faith. He did not know very much about the working classes, but some highly cultivated artisans read his works, and corresponded with him. From them he gathered that the cream of their order, the intellectual aristocracy of labour, were rejecting all religion because they could not believe in miracles, or in the verbal inspiration of the Bible. He thought it a grievous thing that people should squabble over such a question as disestablishment, while the very existence of religion itself was at stake. He therefore proceeded to set forth his own ideas of what reasonable men might hold, and pious men might abandon. Popular theology rested on a mistaken conception of the Bible as a scientific work, whereas the Bible was literary, not scientific, and could not be broken up into propositions, like a manual of logic. Religion was concerned with conduct, and conduct he quaintly defined as three-fourths of human life. Nothing was so easy to understand as conduct, though nothing was harder than always to do right. The truth of religion was not to be proved by morals, nor by metaphysics, but by personal and practical experiment. "He that doeth my will shall know of the doctrine." This view was not original. Among Mr. Arnold's own contemporaries, Dr. Martineau, a member of the despised sect, was never tired of urging it. The definition of religion as "morality touched by emotion" is happy, and the most orthodox Christian might accept it, so far as it goes.

But Mr. Arnold called upon us to reject a good

deal in the hope of saving the rest. The proposition
that "the God of the Universe is a Person" he set
aside as unprofitable and mischievous. God was the
Eternal, and the Eternal was the enduring power, not
ourselves, which makes for righteousness. Therefore
Mr. Arnold, in quoting the Bible, substituted "the
Eternal" for "the Lord," which he regarded, Heaven
knows why, as meaning "a magnified and non-natural
man." The effect upon the ordinary reader, who
knows the Authorised Version almost by heart, is like
suddenly swallowing a fish-bone. Mr. Arnold seems to
have been pleased with "the Eternal" from the mouths
of boys and girls in the Jewish schools he inspected.
But he forgot that, to say nothing of other considerations, in stately and rhythmical English three syllables are very different from one. "Der Aberglaube
ist die Poesie des Lebens," said Goethe; — "Extra belief is the Poetry of Life." Mr. Arnold, who cites this
passage with approval, nevertheless proposes to get rid
of the poetry by the rationalism of faith. He points
out that a belief in the nearness of the Second Advent
was universal among early Christians, including the
Apostles, and that some of the words attributed to
Christ can hardly be construed in any other sense.
He shows that St. Paul interpreted Hebrew prophecy
in a manner which will not bear examination, that
Christ was far above His reporters, who may possibly
have misunderstood Him, and that the Zeit-Geist, the
Time-Spirit, has made belief in miracles impossible.
"The Kingdom of God is within you" was the essence
of the true gospel. The method and secret of Jesus
were repentance and peace. He "restored the intuition" which belonged to Israel, though what this

intuition is does not very clearly appear. "God is
a spirit" means "God is an influence," the influence
which preserves us against faults of temper, and faults
of sensuality. The supposed variance between St.
Paul and St. James is a mistake (here Mr. Arnold becomes unexpectedly orthodox). Works without faith
are as futile as faith without works. "Neither cir-
cumcision availeth anything, nor uncircumcision, but
the keeping of the Commandments of God."

To all which it may of course be said, that Mr.
Arnold could not pick and choose. Christ's teaching
must be taken as a whole, or as we have it. If He
did not say, "Go ye and teach all nations," how do we
know that He said, "I am the resurrection and the
life"? If He did not say, "Destroy this temple, and I
will build it again in three days," how do we know
that He said, "Blessed are the meek"? Once begin
to tamper with the record, and you saw the branch on
which you are sitting between yourself and the tree.
According to this emphatic and uncritical but not
illogical creed, the whole of the New Testament must
stand or fall together. The resurrection cannot indeed
be put on the same footing as the crucifixion, because
the crucifixion is in Tacitus. The miracle of the Gad-
arene swine cannot be bracketed with the Sermon on
the Mount, because the Sermon on the Mount must
have been composed by some one, though the swine
never existed at all, or never left their pastures. But
unless we believe that Christ said exactly what is
attributed to Him in the gospels at the precise time
and in the precise place there given, we must regard
Him as a purely mythical personage. Mr. Arnold
would have replied that Christ did not speak Greek,

the most metaphysical, but Aramaic, the plainest of
languages; that ideas have therefore been imputed to
Him which He never intended; that the authority of
the sayings reported to have been uttered after His
death cannot be as high as if that event had not
occurred; that both the date and the authorship of the
Fourth Gospel are obscure; and that it is a function
of true criticism to reject particular expressions inconsistent with ascertained character or style. He might
have materially strengthened his position (I do not say
that he would have established it) by a comparison of
Christianity and Buddhism as they originally were
with what they afterwards became.

Some of Mr. Arnold's judgments are remarkably
penetrating and shrewd. Such, for instance, is the
description of Frederick Maurice, "that pure and de-
vout spirit, of whom, however, the truth must at last
be said, that in theology he passed his life beating the
bush with deep emotion, and never starting the hare."
So, too, of the three creeds. It may be irreverent, but
it is exceedingly clever from Mr. Arnold's point of
view, to call them popular science, learned science, and
learned science with a strong dash of temper. To Mr.
Arnold all creeds were anathema. He could not away
with them. The Apostles' was as bad as the Nicene,
and the Nicene no better than the Athanasian. Yet
that he never lost his hold upon vital religion is surely
clear from the fine passage on the 102nd page of the
first edition, where he says that though religion makes
for men's happiness, it does not rest upon that as a
motive, but "finds a far surer ground in personal
devotion to Christ, who brought the doctrine to His
disciples and made a passage for it into their hearts;

in believing that Christ is come from God, following
Christ, loving Christ. And in the happiness which
this believing in Him, following Him, and loving
Him gives, it finds the mightiest of sanctions." *Literature and Dogma* never rises to the level of *Ecce
Homo* either in substance or in style. It is less high,
less deep, less penetrating, less sympathetic. But
its moral and intellectual honesty is stamped upon
every page.

The storm which raged round *Literature and Dogma*
found an echo even in the family circle. He had to
defend himself to his sister Fanny, and he did so in
words as unquestionably dignified as they are obvi-
ously sincere. "There is a levity," he says (*Letters*,
vol. ii. page 120), "which is altogether evil ; but to treat
miracles and the common anthropomorphic ideas of God
as what one may lose and yet keep one's hope, courage,
and joy, as what are not really matters of life and
death in the keeping or losing of them, this is desirable
and necessary, if one holds, as I do, that the common
anthropomorphic idea of God and the reliance on
miracles must and will inevitably pass away." That
is an accurate summary of Mr. Arnold's position, which
was further developed in *God and the Bible* (1875).
This work, reprinted from the *Contemporary Review*, is
a sequel to *Literature and Dogma*, and a reply to its
critics. There is no levity in *God and the Bible*, nor is
it entirely destructive. For while the first part aims
at separating Christianity from the God of Miracles
and the God of Metaphysics, the second part is directed
against those German Rationalists who regard the
Fourth Gospel as an elaborate fiction in the style of
Plato. "Religion," says Lord Salisbury in his incisive

way, "can no more be separated from dogma than
light from the sun." And on this point Mr. Gladstone
would have completely agreed with him. But even
the rare concurrence of two political opposites cannot
alter the fact that in all ages of the world's history
dogma has been a matter of indifference, or even of
active dislike, to profoundly religious minds. To
them Mr. Arnold appealed without the fervent piety
of Archbishop Leighton, but at the same time with an
earnest, almost passionate, desire to save spirituality
from the onward rush of materialism. Of the Eu-
hemeristic method, which makes merely quantitative
concession, he speaks with scorn. "It is as if we were
startled by the extravagance of supposing Cinderella's
fairy godmother to have actually changed the pumpkin
into a coach and six, but should suggest that she
really did change it into a one-horse cab." But in his
metaphysical chapter he involves himself in specu-
lations almost as fanciful. He advises his disciples,
the readers who ran *Literature and Dogma* through so
many editions in so short a time, not to use the word
"being," or any of its tenses, when they speak about
God. For the Greek verb εἰμί, it seems, is derived from
a Sanskrit root which signifies the act of breathing,
and is purely phænomenal in the proper sense of that
much abused term. But this is like the discovery,
true or fancied, that the word God means "shining."
Qui hæret in litera hæret in cortice. Etymology only
proves itself. Mr. Arnold makes great play with the
criticism that *Literature and Dogma* was wanting in
"vigour and rigour." But he certainly disposes of
Descartes's *Cogito, ergo sum* in a rigorous and vigorous fashion enough. Self-consciousness is more than

breathing, and no mere philologist can explain it away. Mr. Arnold is on much firmer ground when he deals with the historic materials for the life of Christ. "The record," he says, "when we first get it, has passed through at least half a century or more of oral tradition, and through more than one written account." Mr. Arnold's view, and since his time the learned Professor Harnack's view, of the Fourth Gospel is that St. John was the original source from which the sayings attributed to Christ in it come, but that he did not write the Gospel, that he was not responsible for the form of it, and that spurious sayings, or *logia*, of Christ were mixed up with those which are genuine. "We might," says Mr. Arnold, "go through the Fourth Gospel chapter by chapter, and endeavour to assign to each and all of the *logia* in it their right character—to determine what in them is probably Jesus, and what is the combining, repeating, and expanding Greek editor. But this would be foreign to our object." Vigorous and rigorous enough. But nobody, not even Professor Harnack, can know as much as that. This Greek editor is an imaginary personage. He may have existed, or he may not. Mr. Arnold's service to Biblical criticism lies not in inventing him, but in showing how much more the interpretation of the Bible is a literary than a metaphysical task.

Last Essays on Church and Religion (1877) do what their name implies. They close the chapter of Mr. Arnold's theology, and may fitly close this chapter of mine. They are chiefly interesting for a thoughtful and appropriate study of Bishop Butler, originally delivered in the form of two lectures to the Philo-

sophical Institution at Edinburgh. The effect of these
essays upon my mind is not precisely what Mr. Arnold
intended it to be. " Bishop Butler and the Zeit-Geist "
he called them. The Zeit-Geist in Mr. Arnold's hands,
like the " Être Suprême " in Robespierre's, began to be
a bore. The picture of the great Bishop, or rather of
the great man who happened to be a Bishop, drawn
with Mr. Arnold's winning and prepossessing grace,
allures and at the same time awes the beholder. It
helps me at least to understand the supremacy of
Butler at Oxford in Mr. Arnold's time, and in Mr.
Gladstone's. True it is that Butler did not grapple,
did not pretend to grapple, with the root of the question. He assumed not merely the existence of God,
but the existence of a future life. He laid himself
open to the logically unanswerable reply of Hume,
that more cannot be put into the conclusion than is
contained in the premises, and that therefore a world
constructed by analogy cannot be better than this,
though it may be as good. It is possible that Butler
has made other people atheists besides James Mill.
Mr. Arnold says, truly enough, that the *Analogy* was
aimed at the mob of freethinkers and loose livers who
frequented Queen Caroline's routs, to whom Shaftes-
bury's *Characteristics* were the last word of philosophy.
But if we put aside all that, what a wonderful figure
remains. " To me," says Mr. Goldwin Smith, " an
episcopal philosopher is a philosopher and nothing
more; a dead bishop is a dead man." Granted. But
what a man, and what a philosopher, is Butler. He
walked through the gay throng at St. James's, he
preached to the fashionable congregation at the Rolls'
Chapel like a being from another world. He paid

them no compliments. He offered them no congratulations. He told them the realities of things. "Things are what they are, and the consequences of them will be what they will be; why then should we desire to be deceived?" Like Pascal, he was profoundly impressed with the littleness of human nature, and the vanity of all earthly concerns. He exposed with pitiless accuracy the springs and motives of men's conduct. Without a trace of humour, he made frivolity ridiculous. He almost worshipped reason. Reason, he said, was the only faculty by which we could judge the claims even of Revelation itself. Yet this cold, passionless critic was full of benevolence, abounding in charity to the poor, and so devoted to works of mystical piety that he earned, or at least acquired, the reputation of a Papist. But this is not a life of Bishop Butler.

In the preface to this volume Mr. Arnold is more than usually explicit about his own creed. "I believe," he says, "that Christianity will survive because of its natural truth. Those who fancied that they had done with it, those who had thrown it aside because what was presented to them under its name was so unreceivable, will have to return to it again, and to learn it better." He pleads eloquently for some "great soul" to arise, and purge the ore of Christianity from the dross. "But," as he adds somewhat bitterly, "to rule over the moment and the credulous has more attraction than to work for the future and the sane." It is, however, sometimes rather difficult to know what he would be at. For in his address to the London clergy at Sion College he gravely argues that the State should adopt "some form of religion or other — that which seems best suited to the majority." The London

clergy showed him no little kindness, and politely
made as though they agreed with him. But they
must have been a little staggered by this Parliamentary
view of the faith. It reminds one of the American
who said, in the course of a discussion upon eternal
punishment, "Well, all I can say is, that our people
would never stand it."

A higher conception of the Established Church may
be found on page 37 of these Essays, where he says
that it "is to be considered as a national Christian
society for the promotion of goodness, to which a man
cannot but wish well, and in which he might rejoice to
minister." Mr. Arnold did not write for those who
were satisfied with the popular theology. He wrote
for those who were not. His object was not to disturb
any one's faith, but to convince those who could not
believe in the performance of miracles, or the fulfilment
of prophecies, that they need not therefore become ma-
terialists. He could quote many texts on his side, as
for instance, "Except I do signs and wonders ye will
not believe," and "The Kingdom of God is within
you." The occasional flippancy of *Literature and
Dogma,* however deplorable, is a small thing compared
with the warfare against ignorance and grossness
which Mr. Arnold never ceased to wage.

CHAPTER XII

In politics Matthew Arnold was a Liberal Conservative, which, as Lord John Russell remarked, says in seven syllables what Whig says in one. His patron, Lord Lansdowne, was a Whig of the purest water, equally afraid of moving and of standing still. Mr. Arnold himself was never a candidate for Parliament. Even if he had been disposed to take part in the "Thyestean banquet of clap-trap," his position as a member of the Civil Service would have prevented him. But his practical interest in politics, always keen, increased with age, and during the year before his death he contributed to the *Nineteenth Century* a series of articles on the Session of 1887. When he left off dabbling in theology, politics absorbed him more and more. They promised quicker returns. "Perhaps," he wrote to Mr. Grant Duff, on the 22nd of August 1879, "perhaps we shall end our days in the tail of a rising current of popular religion, both ritual and dogmatic" With that feeling, which I suspect was stronger than the expression of it, Mr. Arnold turned to more mundane matters. No one knew better how to deliver himself, as Shakespeare says, like a man of this world. His long experience of official work had made him thoroughly practical. He had received from nature a keen eye for the central point of a case, and a power of lucid exposition which is the most formidable of all arguments. Of working men, as I have said, he knew very little, though many of them read and appreciated his books. But with the upper and middle classes of society, their principles and prejudices, their faults and failings, he was thoroughly well acquainted. Nothing in his life is more honourable to him than the persistent efforts which he made, for more than twenty years, to get a decent system of secondary education established in this country. Only now, when he has been dead nearly fourteen years, is this question being really taken up in a practical spirit by a responsible Government. On the other hand, he seldom mentions political dissenters, whose importance he recognised, except in terms of caricature; and of the great driving force which, apart from his more conspicuous accomplishments, Mr. Gladstone wielded, he had a most imperfect idea. He took the superficial view of Whig coteries that the author of the Irish Land Acts, and the greatest financier of the age, was a rhetorical sophist, a man of words and phrases, not of business and its execution. This view finds frequent utterance in the second volume of the published *Letters*. The piety or prudence of Mr. George Russell has in most instances suppressed the name of his former chief; but a schoolboy far less intelligent than Macaulay's would find no difficulty in filling the blank.

Mr. Arnold's first incursion into practical politics was not a fortunate one. He was a strong, almost a fanatical, opponent of the Burials Bill. He did not take the line, logically unassailable, that an Established Church comprises the whole nation, that all its rites, including the Burial Service, are national, and that

as Dissenters were entitled to burial in national
cemeteries with national rites, they had no grievance.
If he had been a true Erastian, that is what he would
have said. But he chose to argue that the permission
of other services would produce scandal, would be, as
he repeated about fifty times, like the substitution
for a reading from Milton of a reading from Eliza
Cook. The twenty-three years that have elapsed since
the Burials Bill received the Royal assent have completely falsified this gloomy prediction. No statute
has worked more smoothly. Even the foolish clergymen who discovered to their delight that it did not com-
pel them to let the bell be tolled for a schismatic have
long since ceased to excite any interest. That the Act
is inconsistent with the principle of an Established
Church seems to me clear. But the people of England,
though just, are not logical, and the removal of this
grievance, which was really part of a much larger one,
made the larger one more difficult to redress. Like
many freethinkers, Mr. Arnold had a horror of disestablishment. He was opposed to it even in Ireland,
where the nature of things might be said to demand
it. The last fifteen years have vindicated his belief
that in England public opinion was against it, and
that the political power of Nonconformity was on the
decline.

Mr. Arnold's volume of *Mixed Essays* — an unhappy
title, suggesting biscuits — contains two or three which
may be classed as political, and which are therefore
fit to be treated here. " Equality " is an elaborate
argument, which never took any hold upon the
English people, against freedom of bequest. Mr.
Arnold had the support of Mill, but he had not the

support of the public.   He saw clearly enough that
the Real Estates Intestacy Bill, with which Liberals
used to play, would have had no practical result, for a
man who wanted to defeat it had only to make a will.
There is much to be said for his case.   The earth, as
Turgot put it, belongs to the living, and not to the
dead.   It is no infringement of human liberty to
prevent a man from fettering those who come after
him.   But this is a subject on which the most eloquent
and the most profound philosophers would contend in
vain with the customs and instincts of the English
people.   They did not mind Lord Cairns's Settled Land
Act, which enables the owner of a life interest in land
to sell it if he invests the money for the benefit of the
reversioner.   They would perhaps tolerate the complete
abolition of all limited ownership in land.   But of the
compulsory division of property after death, which prevails on the Continent, they will not hear.   Mr. Arnold
tells an amusing story of an American who was asked
what could be done in the United States, with its freedom
of bequest, if a great landed estate were strictly entailed.
The American replied, with more humour than candour,
that the will could be set aside on the ground of
insanity.   Such is the difference of sentiment between
the old country and the new.   In this case Mr. Arnold
rode his hobby too hard.   The feudal origin of our
land laws is indisputable, and their practical incon-
veniences are numerous.   Yet it is not freedom of
bequest, it is influences far more subtle and profound,
which have " the natural and necessary effect under
present circumstances of materialising our upper
class, vulgarising our middle class, and brutalising
our lower class."   But, indeed, vulgarity is confined

to no class.   It is, and always must be, a property of
the individual.

  " I do not," Mr. Arnold wrote (*Mixed Essays*, 2nd Ed.
p. 108), " I do not profess to be a politician, but simply
one of a disinterested class of observers, who, with no
organised and embodied set of supporters to please, set
themselves to observe honestly and to report faithfully
the state and prospects of our civilisation." This passage,
which fairly and modestly describes himself, is taken
from his admirable essay on " Irish Catholicism and
British Liberalism," in which Mr. Bright entirely con-
curred. Unlike freedom of bequest, this subject is full
of vivid interest and high import at the present time.
An Irish Catholic University, for which Mr. Arnold
pleads, is the subject of the best and most thoughtful
speeches Mr. Balfour has ever delivered. It is a point
upon which he and Mr. Morley quite agree. A Royal
Commission was appointed to consider it last year, and
though no Government will take it up, it has enlisted
the sympathies of eminent men on both sides of
politics. The question is beset with difficulties, and
cannot be settled offhand by any formula. One of
these difficulties is how a Catholic University should
be defined. For Trinity College, Dublin, is a Catholic
University in the sense that it admits Catholics, if only
they would go there. And for a Catholic University
endowed with public money but inaccessible to Protestants nobody asks. Mr. Arnold answers the question in a sentence.   " I call Strasburg a Protestant
and Bonn a Catholic University in this sense : that
religion and the matters mixed up with religion are
taught in the one by Protestants and in the other by
Catholics."   In this essay Mr. Arnold intimates his

opinion that "the prevailing form for the Christianity
of the future will be the form of Catholicism; but a
Catholicism purged, opening itself to the light and
air, having the consciousness of its own poetry, freed
from its sacerdotal despotism, and freed from its
psuedo-scientific apparatus of superannuated dogma."
It hardly seems probable.   But the curtains of the future hang.   The Professors in Mr. Arnold's University
would be "nominated and removed not by the bishops,
but by a responsible minister of State acting for the
Irish nation itself."   A minister of what State?   This
simple question, which Mr. Arnold does not answer,
raises the whole issue of Home Rule.   Mr. Arnold was
very anxious that a religious census should be taken
in England, as it is in Ireland.   In Ireland everybody
is either a Catholic or a Protestant, and nobody
attempts to conceal which he is, bad as his Protestantism or his Catholicism may be.   In England such a
census would be fallacious, because persons holding
Matthew Arnold's religious opinions would describe
themselves on the census-paper as Churchmen.

In three essays, besides his official Reports, Mr.
Arnold pleaded earnestly for the establishment in the
United Kingdom of secondary or intermediate schools.
One of them is in *Mixed Essays*, the other is in *Irish
Essays*, of which I shall have more to say in connection
with Ireland.   One of them is called " An Unregarded
Irish Grievance."   The other two have the quaint
titles taken from the Vulgate, of which Matthew
Arnold was almost as fond as Bacon, " Porro unum est
necessarium," — " But one Thing is Needful "; and
" Ecce Convertimur ad Gentes," — " Lo, we turn to the
Gentiles."   This last was a lecture delivered to the

Working Men's College at Ipswich, and the Gentiles
were the working classes, whose interest in the subject
Mr. Arnold wished to arouse. All these essays deserve
the most careful study.   They were written by a
master of his subject, they are as full of knowledge as
of zeal, they are eminently practical, and they have
the most direct bearing upon the politics of the day.
The course of events has in this matter fully justified
Mr. Arnold, who was wiser than the statesmen, and
ahead of his time.   In his address at Ipswich he took
another dip into the future which also showed his pre-
science.   "No one in England," he said, "seems to
imagine that municipal government is applicable
except in towns."   And he went on to suggest the
policy, since carried out by both political parties, in
the form of County and District and Parish Councils.

In the preface to *Irish Essays*, dated 1882, Mr.
Arnold says that "practical politicians and men of the
world are apt rather to resent the incursion of a man
of letters into the field of politics."   They only resent
it when he does not take their side.   Both Unionists
and Home Rulers were always boasting of their
literary supporters in the great controversy of 1886.
But it must be admitted that the wise men of the
study do not always see further ahead than the mere
politicians of the market-place.   Writing, in French,
to M. Fontanès on the 22nd of September 1882, Mr.
Arnold says, "The English army will leave Egypt."
The process of departure has been slow.

Whatever Mr. Arnold wrote about Ireland is worth
serious attention.   He took for his master Burke,
perhaps the greatest intellect of the eighteenth century, certainly the greatest intellect concerned with

Irish affairs. For Burke, though an expatriated Irishman, never lost his love of Ireland, and understood
her thoroughly. Himself a Protestant, his wife was a
Catholic, as his mother had been, and though he had
plenty of bigotry in politics, from religious bigotry he
was free. The great change produced upon him by
events in France did not affect his Irish policy, and to
the day of his death he supported Catholic Emancipation. Whether, if he had lived three years longer, he
would have been in favour of a Union, we cannot certainly tell. That he would not have voted for it without emancipation we may be sure. Mr. Arnold, I
think, failed to appreciate the greatness of the reform
effected by the Land Act of 1881. But his acute
analysis of its influence upon Irish opinion is quite in
Burke's manner. Ministers, he says, declared their
belief that there were very few extortionate landlords
in Ireland. But the Act has led to a general reduc-
tion of rents. Therefore the Irish people will say
"We owe you no thanks; you have done us justice
without meaning it. You could not help it, our case
was so strong." "Burke," says Mr. Arnold, truly and
finely, "Burke is, it seems to me, the greatest of
English statesmen in this sense at any rate: that he is
the only one who traces the reason of things in politics
and enables us to trace it too." Mr. Arnold aimed at
following that good example, and when he failed, it
was because he had not, like Burke, the political
training which no amount of cleverness can altogether
supply. In one of the two essays on "The Incom-
patibles" he says, acutely enough, "Our aristocratic
class does not firmly protest against the unfair treatment of Irish Catholicism, because it is nervous about

the land. Our middle class does not firmly insist
on breaking with the old evil system of Irish land-
lordism, because it is nervous about Popery." In the
other he says that the English are "just, but not
amiable," which, if not strictly and literally true, is at
least worth thinking about. But, on the other hand,
it was not practical politics, nor yet common sense, to
suggest that instead of giving Irish tenants fair rent,
free sale, and fixity of tenure, Irish landlords should
be bought out if, in the opinions of Lord Coleridge
and Mr. Samuel Morley, they deserved to be. Mr.
Arnold's essay on Copyright is chiefly remarkable for
its advocacy of international copyright with the United
States on terms since obtained, and its repudiation of
Lord Farrer's theory, supported by Mr. Gladstone, that
authors could rely upon royalties. But "The Future
of Liberalism" contains what seems to me a fundamental misconception on Mr. Arnold's part, and a
fruitful parent of error. "In general," he says, "the
mind of the country is, as I have already said, profoundly Liberal." Mr. Arnold was apt to think, with
the bellman in the *Hunting of the Snark*, that what he
told you three times was true. England is not profoundly Liberal, and never was. She is profoundly
Conservative, and always has been. There was an out-
burst of Liberalism in the early Thirties, caused partly
by the Revolution of 1830 in France, and partly by
the intolerable absurdities of our representative system. Mr. Gladstone had the power of rousing extraordinary enthusiasm on behalf of particular policies
at particular times. But these are the exceptions to
the rule, which is patient acquiescence in things as
they are. That is why most of the wisest English-

men have been Liberals. There is no risk of too rapid progress in England. The danger is the other way.

It must, I think, be reckoned one of the few misfortunes in a most happy life that Matthew Arnold should have been tempted to visit America as a public lecturer. No doubt the temptation was great. Mr. Arnold's means were moderate, and he had to provide for his family as well as for himself. His own tastes were of the simplest, and he was the most contented of men. But a large sum of money was a consideration to him, while both he and his wife had always been fond of travelling. So in the autumn of 1883 they went. Of course they were most warmly greeted, and most hospitably entertained. But the lecturing was not a success. Major Pond, in his *Eccentricities of Genius*, says, " Matthew Arnold came to this country and gave one hundred lectures. Nobody ever heard any of them, not even those sitting in the front row." He adds that General Grant, who attended the first lecture in Chickering Hall, New York, was overheard to say after a few minutes, " Well, wife, we have paid to see the British lion; we cannot hear him roar, so we had better go home." This explains a passage in Mr. Arnold's letter to his sister Fanny, dated the 8th of November 1883, in which the General is represented as calling at the office of the *Tribune* " to thank them for their good report of the main points of my lecture, as he had thought the line taken so very important, but had heard imperfectly." Although he had been a Professor at Oxford, Mr. Arnold was not accustomed to address crowded audiences in large halls, and he did not understand the management of **his voice.** He took lessons in elocution at Boston, but at the age of sixty it was late to learn, and the thing was not in his line. He took it, as he took everything, with invincible cheerfulness and good-humour. But it has a rather grotesque effect to read in a letter to his younger daughter, written from the Union Club, Chicago, on the 21st of January 1884, " We have had a week of good houses (I consider myself now as an actor, for my managers take me about with theatrical tickets, at reduced rates, over the railways, and the tickets have *Matthew Arnold troupe* printed on them)." Lord Coleridge and Sir Henry Irving, who were both there at the same time with him, were both in their respective places, but one feels that Matthew Arnold was out of place. He enjoyed himself of course, — he always did. I remember the delight with which he told me of his invitation from Mr. Phineas Barnum, " the greatest showman on earth." " You, Mr. Arnold," wrote the great man, " are a celebrity, I am a notoriety ; we ought to be acquainted." " I couldn't go," remarked Mr. Arnold, " but it was very nice of him." Matthew Arnold told Mr. George Russell that *Discourses in America,* published by Macmillan in 1885, was the book of all others by which he should most wish to be remembered. It consists of three lectures, but the only one which can be called political is the first, on " Numbers, or the Majority and the Remnant." The argument of this essay is as follows. The majority are always wrong ; the remnant are always right. Isaiah represented the remnant of Israel ; Plato represented the remnant of Athens. In both cases the State was so small that the remnant were not numerous enough to do any good. In the United States the population is so large

that the remnant must be sufficient, and the United
States are therefore safe. I cannot suppose that this
was anything but elaborate irony on Mr. Arnold's
part, or that his more intelligent hearers were unconscious of the fact. But there were many digres-
sions. It is here that he rebukes his old friends the
French for their worship of "the great goddess Lubric-
ity," called by the Greeks Aselgeia, and describes
Victor Hugo in one of his least felicitous phrases as
"the average sensual man impassioned and grandilo-
quent." The greatest of French dramatists since
Molière is singularly free from the fault which Mr.
Arnold here reprehends.

This was not Mr. Arnold's last visit to the United
States, where his elder daughter married and settled.
He went there again in 1886, and arrived at the
singular conclusion that all the best opinion of
America, the opinion of the "remnant," was hostile
to the Irish policy of Mr. Gladstone. Truly the
eye sees what it brings with it the power of seeing.
This is not the place in which to discuss whether
Home Rule for Ireland would be a good thing or a
bad. That the majority of intelligent and cultivated
Americans thought it in 1886, as they think it now,
to be a good thing, there can be no doubt whatever.
Although he had American friends, whom he valued
and appreciated, Mr. Arnold did not altogether like
America. In the *Nineteenth Century* for April 1888,
the year and month of his death, may be seen his
final judgment on the subject. He had written the
year before for his nephew, Mr. Edward Arnold,
then editor of *Murray's Magazine*, two articles on
the rather dull Memoirs of General Grant, whom, in

one of his freaks of waywardness, he pronounced
superior to Lincoln. Lincoln, it seems, the author
of the speech at Gettysburg and the Second Inaugural, had no "distinction." Happy the nation where
such classic eloquence is not distinguished. Mr. Arnold's last word on American life is the word "unin-
teresting." "The mere nomenclature of the country
acts upon a cultivated person like the incessant
pricking of pins." The "funny man" is a "national
misfortune." So he is here. And, after all, Mark
Twain is better than Ally Sloper. Mr. Arnold's
criticism of what was unsound in American institutions and manners would have been more effective
if he had had, like Mr. Bryce, more sympathy with
what was sound in them.

Any survey of Matthew Arnold's politics would
be incomplete without a reference to his opinions
on Home Rule. To Mr. Gladstone's Home Rule
Bill of 1886 he was decidedly opposed. Both before
and after the General Election of that year he
wrote to the *Times* a strong protest against the
policy embodied in it. These letters, except for
the personal animosity to Mr. Gladstone which the
second displays, are wholly admirable in tone and
temper. In them Mr. Arnold admits to the full
the grievances of Ireland against England, and calls
for their redress. Only he would redress them, not
by a "separate Parliament," but by a "rational and
equitable system of government." Lord Salisbury's
policy of coercion suited him as little as Mr. Gladstone's policy of repeal. He proposed that the local
government of Ireland should be thoroughly over-
hauled and made truly popular, even before such a

system was introduced into the rest of the United
Kingdom.   These letters show the Whig spirit at
its best, and are thoroughly characteristic of Mr.
Arnold.   He followed them up the next year with
three articles in the *Nineteenth Century* called respectively "The Zenith of Conservatism," "Up to Easter,"
and "From Easter to August."   In these, while giving
a general support to the Government of Lord Salisbury, he showed himself to be a very bad Unionist
from the strictly orthodox point of view; for he proposed that there should be not a single Irish Parliament, but two Irish Parliaments, of which one should
legislate for the North and the other for the South.
The fact is, it was not Home Rule, but Gladstone's
Home Rule, that Matthew Arnold disliked.   Indeed,
one might almost say that it was not Home Rule, but
Gladstone.

CHAPTER XIII

THE AFTERMATH

DURING the last twenty years of his life Matthew
Arnold wrote very little poetry; but the little he did
write was very good. There are lines in " Westminster
Abbey " which he never surpassed, and a few which,
in my opinion, he never equalled. This beautiful
poem was composed in memory of Dean Stanley, and
it could have had no worthier subject. For Stanley,
Mr. Arnold's lifelong friend, was not merely the
courtly ecclesiastic, the scholarly divine; he was the
chivalrous defender of all causes and of all persons,
however unpopular for the moment, that stood for
freedom, charity, and truth. If the spirit of Dean
Stanley had always dominated the Establishment, the
Liberation Society would never have been formed.
The chapter in Mrs. Besant's *Autobiography* describing
Dr. Stanley is a noble picture of what a Christian
minister should be. He delighted in all the traditions
of his Abbey, and Mr. Arnold happily chose to connect
with him the beautiful legend which tells of its mystic
consecration by St. Peter himself. In spite of the
fact that these sonorous stanzas recall Milton's great
Ode on the Nativity, they are not disappointing; they
have the note of the grand style —

> " Rough was the winter eve ;
> Their craft the fishers leave,

> And down over the Thames the darkness drew.
>   One still lags last, and turns, and eyes the Pile
>   Huge in the gloom, across in Thorney Isle,
> King Sebert's work, the wondrous Minster new.
>   — 'Tis Lambeth now, where then
> They moor'd their boats among the bulrush stems ;
>   And that new Minster in the matted fen
> The world-famed Abbey by the westering Thames.''

These verses deserve to be called Miltonic, even if they have not the inimitable touch of the master.

But it is the later lines about Demophoon, "the charm'd babe of the Eleusinian king," which I should be disposed to select as the high-water mark of Matthew Arnold's poetry. They haunt the memory with that ineffaceable charm which belongs only to the highest order of poetical expression —

> " The Boy his nurse forgot,
>   And bore a mortal lot.
> Long since, his name is heard on earth no more.
>   In some chance battle on Cithæron's side
>   The nursling of the Mighty Mother died,
> And went where all his fathers went before.''

Here one might well take leave of Matthew Arnold's poems, and pass to those literary essays which he wrote in the full maturity of his knowledge and his power. For, happy in so many things, he was happiest of all in this, that no bodily sense, and no mental faculty, ever suffered in him the smallest abatement. But I cannot omit all mention of the pretty, facile lyrics in which he paid tribute to his beloved dogs and birds. I refer, of course, to "Geist's Grave," to "Poor Matthias," and to "Kaiser Dead." Geist was a Dachshund, Kaiser a mixture of Dachshund and collie.

Matthias was a canary. "Geist's Grave," is by far the
best of the three, and contains at least two excellent
stanzas —

> " That loving heart, that patient soul,
>   Had they indeed no longer span,
>   To run their course, and reach their goal,
>   And read their homily to man ?

> " That liquid, melancholy eye,
>   From whose pathetic, soul-fed springs
>   Seem'd surging the Virgilian cry,
>   The sense of tears in mortal things."

The literary criticism produced by Mr. Arnold in
the last ten years of his life possesses the highest
interest and value.   It ranges over a great variety of
topics, it represents the writer's profoundest mind, it
comes next after his poetry in a comparative estimate
of what he left to the world.   In dealing with politics,
or with theology, Mr. Arnold never moved with the
same ease as in the realm of pure literature, which
was his own.   He loved to take a book, like Mr. Stopford Brooke's excellent *Primer of English Literature*,
and in criticising it to express his own opinions.   He
protested, quite justly, and by no means unnecessarily,
against the foolish idolatry which admires without
discrimination everything in a volume labelled
"Shakespeare."   For it is certain that if Shakespeare
wrote all the plays and all the scenes attributed to
him, he wrote some very poor stuff.   But when Mr.
Arnold says of him, not in substance for the first or
last time, " He is the richest, the most wonderful, the
most powerful, the most delightful of poets; he is not
altogether, nor even eminently, an artist " (*Mixed
Essays*, 2nd Ed. p. 194), he provokes antagonism.

M

There is more in the sonnets than art could have put there. But poems more consummately artistic never came from a human brain and heart. It is, however, a fascinating essay, this on Mr. Brooke's *Primer*, and so is another in the same volume on Falkland, the famous Lord Falkland immortalised by Clarendon. Yet Falkland is perhaps not most judiciously praised (and highly does Mr. Arnold praise him) by comparing him with Bolingbroke, whose levity and insincerity are not redeemed by the false glitter of his meretricious style. Mr. Arnold is severe on Burke for asking " Who now reads Bolingbroke ? " But on this point the popular verdict is with Burke, and I am not prepared to say that it is wrong. Mr. Disraeli did his best for Bolingbroke's public character, and for the principles of " The Patriot King." But, as Dr. Pusey said of Lord Westbury and eternal punishment, he had a personal interest in the question. In " A French Critic on Milton " and " A French Critic on Goethe," Mr. Arnold took up the cudgels for the highly intelligent and respectable M. Scherer. M. Scherer, however, was dull, he was prosy, and even Matthew Arnold could not make him anything else. When this senator of France, and director of the *Temps* newspaper, tells us that *Paradise Lost* is " a false poem, a grotesque poem, a tiresome poem," we can only smile compassionately, and wonder what resemblance to Sainte-Beuve Mr. Arnold could find in M. Scherer. M. Scherer certainly seems to have misled Mr. Arnold on one point of some importance connected with Goethe. Goethe did indeed tell an Italian that " he thought the *Inferno* abominable, the *Purgatorio* dubious, and the *Paradiso* tire-

some." But that was not Goethe's serious opinion.
He made the remark as the surest way to get rid of
an intolerable bore. *Sic me servavit Apollo.* Even
Dante need not object to fulfilling the same functions
as the god of light. How thoroughly Matthew Arnold
himself appreciated Goethe, how much he learned from
him, we all know. His final judgment (*Mixed Essays*,
2nd Ed. p. 311) is contained in two short sentences.
"It is by no means as the greatest of poets that he
deserves the pride and praise of his German countrymen. It is as the clearest, the largest, the most
helpful thinker of modern times." No essay in this
volume is more charming than the memorial tribute
to George Sand. George Sand is, I believe, out of
fashion in France. She is certainly not half so much
read in England as she was twenty years ago. So far
as her best and simplest books are concerned, this is
a great loss. For, as Mr. Arnold so happily quotes
from her, she gives better than almost any one else
"*le sentiment de la vie idéale, qui n'est autre que la vie
normale telle que nous sommes appelés à la connaître,*"
— "the sentiment of the ideal life, which is none
other than the normal life as we are destined to know
it." George Sand never brought the ideal down to the
level of the real.

Oddly bound up with *Irish Essays* are a lecture
to Eton boys on the value of the classics, and an
ingenious disquisition on the French Play in London.
At Eton, where Mr. Arnold believed, or pretended to
believe, that a scientific training was the vogue, he
tracked Greek life through many of its phases by
means of the words εὐτράπελος and εὐτραπελία, to which
perhaps the nearest English equivalents are "versatile"

and "versatility." How εὐτράπελος, a handy man, came to mean βωμολόχος, a lick-spittle, is a long story, and it is curious that, as Mr. Arnold points out, Pindar, in whose Odes it first occurs, uses it in a bad sense, like St. Paul, who applies it to the jesting which is not convenient. In Plato, however, it sometimes has an unfavourable meaning too, and this Mr. Arnold omits to observe. But the value of his lecture lies in its fruitful and suggestive comparison of Greek life with English. No man knew the classics better than Mr. Arnold. No man made a better use of his knowledge. The essay on the French Play is interesting in many ways, not least for the personal reminiscence with which he introduces the subject. " I remember," he says, " how in my youth, after a first sight of the divine Rachel at the Edinburgh Theatre in the part of Hermione, I followed her to Paris, and for two months never missed one of her representations " (*Irish Essays*, Pop. Ed. p. 151). Of course after that Mr. Arnold could not be expected to go into raptures over Mademoiselle Sarah Bernhardt, and he does not. " Something is wanting, or, at least, not present in sufficient force. . . . It was here that Rachel was so great ; she began, one says to oneself as one recalls her image and dwells upon it, — she began almost where Mademoiselle Sarah Bernhardt ends " (page 153). But Mr. Arnold never saw Sarah Bernhardt in *Hamlet*. Again in this essay Mr. Arnold attacks Victor Hugo, and attacks him where, if he sins, he sins in excellent company. " M. Victor Hugo's brilliant gift for versification is exercised within the limits of a form inadequate for true tragic poetry, and by its very presence excluding it " (page 164). That is very dogmatic criticism indeed.

Mr. Arnold disliked the French Alexandrine, even as handled by such a master as Racine, and therefore he pronounced it inadequate for true tragedy. He would not have cared much for a criticism of Homer by a man who disliked hexameters, and thought them inadequate for epic poetry. At page 166 he makes the acute remark that "we have no modern drama, because our vast society is not at present homogeneous enough." Nevertheless he pleads for a national theatre. We shall have a national drama first. Mr. Arnold was an old playgoer, and wrote some lively dramatic notices for the *Pall Mall Gazette* in that name. But the enormous number of Englishmen who do not care for the play, and never go to it, would hardly like to be taxed for theatrical purposes.

The second series of *Essays in Criticism* appeared after Mr. Arnold's death, with a Prefatory Note by Lord Coleridge. But they were collected by himself, and are what he deliberately judged to be worthy of republication. They are nine in number, but the last three do not, I think, add much to the value of the collection. The first six, on the other hand, are equal, if not superior, to any other critical work of Mr. Arnold's. "The Study of Poetry," with which the volume opens, was originally written for Mr. Humphry Ward's *Selections from the English Poets*. It contains Mr. Arnold's final and deliberate judgment upon the true nature of poetry. After quoting Aristotle's "profound observation" that poetry is both a more philosophical thing, and a more serious thing, than history, he says (page 121) that "the substance and matter of the best poetry acquire their special character from possessing, in an eminent degree, truth and serious-

ness." But "the superior character of truth and
seriousness, in the matter and substance of the best
poetry, is inseparable from the superiority of diction
and movement marking its style and manner." Little
can be added to this, and certainly nothing can be
subtracted from it. Next to it, the most interesting
part of the essay is the free and candid estimate of
Burns. This is the more welcome because, while he
was writing the paper, in November 1880, he told his
sister (*Letters*, vol. ii. p. 184) that Burns was "a beast
with splendid gleams." What would Mr. Arnold have
thought of the Philistine who described Catullus as a
beast with splendid gleams ? And yet Catullus, who
was far grosser than Burns, is the poet whom, as the
late Professor Sellar showed, Burns most resembles.
In his beautiful address on Milton, delivered at St.
Margaret's Church, Westminster, a few weeks before
his death, Mr. Arnold said, with truth, force, and
insight (page 66), "In our race are thousands of
readers, presently there will be millions, who know
not a word of Greek and Latin, and will never learn
those languages. If this host of readers are ever to
gain any sense of the power and charm of the great
poets of antiquity, their way to gain it is not through
translations of the ancients, but through the original
poetry of Milton, who has the like power and charm,
because he has the like great style." Only a born man
of letters could have written that. But when Mr.
Arnold quotes from Gray's friend, Dr. Warton, the
words, "He never spoke out," and says that "in these
four words is contained the whole history of Gray,
both as a man and as a poet," he becomes fantastic.
What Dr. Warton means, is that Gray was not com-

municative about the state of his own health. He
was a copious letter-writer, and his letters are among
the best in the language. If the amount of his poetry
is comparatively small, it had a range wide enough
to include the " Progress of Poesy," the "Elegy in a
Country Churchyard," and the political satires. To
Keats, Mr. Arnold became juster as he grew older,
and in this his final estimate he couples him, not with
Maurice de Guérin, but with Shakespeare. This
reminds one of Lord Young's comment on the remark
that Barnes, the Dorset poet, might be put on the
same shelf with Burns. "It would have to be a long
shelf," said the witty Judge. But it is true that "no
one else in English poetry, save Shakespeare, has in
expression quite the fascinating felicity of Keats, his
perfection of loveliness " (page 119). The essay on
Wordsworth is so good, that to praise it is better than
to criticise it, and to read it is better than either. But
such a statement as that " the *Excursion* and the
Prelude, his poems of greatest bulk, are by no means
Wordsworth's best work " (page 135) requires a justification which Mr. Arnold does not give it. It would
be difficult to find in any of Wordsworth's shorter
pieces better verses than the lines on the Simplon
Pass, or the passage beginning "Fabric it seemed of
diamond and of gold." While, however, I cannot
help thinking that Mr. Arnold exaggerates the prosi-
ness of Wordsworth's prosaic passages, and dwells too
much upon that familiar theme, he more than com-
pensates for any trifling blemishes by such a noble
sentence as this : " His expression may often be called
bald, as, for instance, in the poem of *Resolution and
Independence ;* but it is bald as the bare mountain tops

are bald, with a baldness which is full of grandeur." Mr. Arnold is readier to do Byron justice than most Wordsworthians are. It was Tennyson that Wordsworth prevented him from appreciating, not Byron. Byron's poetry seems, so far as one can judge, to be out of date now. It is his letters rather than his poems which people read. But his "sincerity and strength," to use the phrase which Mr. Arnold quotes from Mr. Swinburne, must always be acknowledged.

The remaining essays in this volume deal with Professor Dowden's *Life of Shelley*, with the earlier writings of Count Tolstoi, and with the *Diary of Amiel*. Mr. Arnold was profoundly disgusted with the details of Shelley's private life, with "Godwin's house of sordid horror," with Byron's "brutal selfishness," and so on. "What a set! what a world!" he exclaims naturally enough. To compare them with the Oriel Common Room shows perhaps a lack in the sense of proportion. They are more like the strange company who accompanied Candide on his rambles. But after Professor Dowden's strange apologetics, Mr. Arnold's rational morals and inbred sense of refinement are salutary and refreshing. To say of Shelley as a poet that he is "a beautiful and ineffectual angel, beating in the void his luminous wings in vain," is impressive and I suppose it means something. But it does not account for the "Skylark," or "When the Lamp is Shattered," or the mighty "Ode to the West Wind." Mr. Arnold's analysis of *Anna Karenina* is appreciative enough, and he would have thoroughly enjoyed *Resurrection* if he had lived to read it. But his recommendation that Count Tolstoi should leave religion and stick to literature, comes strangely from

the author of *Literature and Dogma*.   No living writer
has inculcated the teaching of Christ with more
eloquence than Count Tolstoi.   Of Amiel, it is no
doubt true that he shines more in literary criticism
than in mystic speculation.   He could hardly shine
less.   But what had Matthew Arnold to do with
Amiel?

CHAPTER XIV

CONCLUSION

So early as October 1882, Mr. Arnold, in an amusing letter to Mr. Morley, spoke of resignation. "I announced yesterday at the office my intention of retiring at Easter or Whitsuntide. Gladstone will never promote the author of *Literature and Dogma* if he can help it, and meanwhile my life is drawing to an end, and I have no wish to execute the Dance of Death in an elementary school" (*Letters*, ii. 207). He did not, however, actually resign till the 30th of April 1886, when he had been an Inspector for thirty-five years. Mr. Gladstone did not promote the author of *Literature and Dogma*. But he offered him a pension of two hundred and fifty pounds, "as a public recognition of service to the poetry and literature of England." After some quite unnecessary hesitation, Mr. Arnold accepted the offer. Few men, to say nothing of poetry and literature, ever served the public more faithfully for a remuneration which at no time equalled the salary of a police magistrate or a County Court judge. If he did not work so hard as some of his colleagues at the routine and drudgery of inspection, his reports are the most luminous, the most interesting, and the most suggestive that have ever been issued from the Education Department. A collection of these Reports from 1852 to 1882 was published by Messrs. Macmillan in 1889, with an introduction from the pen of the late Lord Sandford, so long Secretary to the Education Office.

In the autumn of 1885, Mr. Arnold was sent to inquire into the working of elementary education in Germany, France, and Switzerland. He was especially directed to report upon the payment of fees by the parent, by the municipality, and by the State. This Report is not quite so good a piece of composition as its predecessors, and there are signs that it was written in a hurry. His own recommendations are characteristic. He thought that the balance of argument was against free education. But he held that it had better be given because the want of it put a powerful weapon in the hands of the agitator. This is thoroughly and essentially Whig. He concluded by urging once more that secondary education should be organised, as it seems likely at last to be. Free education was adopted three years after his death.

This Report was Mr. Arnold's last bit of official work. After his resignation he used his freedom to write more on politics, and his pen was never idle. His general health was good, though he had been warned of hereditary weakness in the heart which made any sudden or violent exertion dangerous. While at Liverpool with his wife on Sunday the 15th of April 1888, he ran to catch a tramcar, and died in a moment. He had gone to meet his elder daughter on her way home from the United States, and in the delighted expectation of seeing her he passed away. Few knew anything of his malady, and no one looked less like an invalid. He was sixty-five at the time of his death, but he might easily have passed for a much younger man. His eye was not dim, nor his natural force abated. Always full of gaiety and good-humour, he had the high spirits of a boy, and the serene contentment of a philosopher. Keenly as he appreciated the enjoyments of life, being fastidious in taste and something of an epicure, his wants were few and soon satisfied. He was the most sociable, the most lovable, the most companionable of men. Perhaps the function in which he shone least was that of a public speaker. I only heard him once, but the occasion was sufficiently remarkable to be worth notice. It was the Jubilee of the Oxford Union in 1873. Matthew Arnold had never, so far as I am aware, anything to do with the Union. But almost every Oxford man in the front rank of public life, except Mr. Gladstone, attended the dinner, including Lord Chancellor Selborne, who presided, Archbishop Tait, Cardinal Manning, Lord Salisbury, and Sir John Duke Coleridge. Mr. Arnold was to respond for Literature, which had been proposed by that accomplished orator, Dr. Liddon. But whether he was unwell, or whether he disliked Liddon's urbane irony, he replied in a single sentence rather too sarcastic for the occasion, and not worth reproducing at this distance of time.

It is impossible to read through Mr. Arnold's books and letters without feeling that he was a good man in the best sense of that term. His character was a singularly engaging one, and it rested upon solid virtues which are less common than amiability. A better son, husband, father, there could not be. His moral standard was much the same as Dr. Arnold's, and how high that was everybody knows. In religious matters he departed very widely from the school of thought in which he had been reared. That he was himself a sincerely religious man, and deeply interested in religious questions, it is impossible to doubt. But his religion was so peculiar that it can scarcely have much permanent influence upon mankind. Christianity without miracles, and without dogmatic theology, is not only practicable, but has sufficed for some of the best Christians that ever lived. It is probably the religion of most educated laymen in the Church of England to-day. But Christianity without a personal God, without anything more definite than a tendency not ourselves which makes for righteousness, seems to have neither past nor future. It is, in the language of the book which, with all his learning, Mr. Arnold knew best, salt which has lost his savour. Mr. Arnold's unfortunate habit of quoting the Bible in a translation of his own deprived the passages so rendered of their hold upon the English mind. His contributions to pure literature, on the other hand, seem secure of a permanent place in the shelves and the minds of Englishmen. Mr. Arnold, as we have seen, had his critical limitations. He excluded too much. But judging his critical work, as talent should be judged, at its best, one can hardly overpraise it. It is original, penetrating, lucid, sympathetic, and just. Of all modern poets, except Goethe, he was the best critic. Of all modern critics, with the same exception, he was the best poet. No one, not even Mr. Lecky, more abounds in telling and appropriate quotations. As a poet he ranks only below the greatest of all. Though he felt the influence of Wordsworth, he was no imitator. He was a voice, not an echo. A popular

poet, as Byron was, as Tennyson is, he never was, and
is never likely to be.   He may almost be said to have
written for University men, and, as we may say nowadays, for University women.   As a critic he was incapable of obscurity or of inaccuracy.   His scholarship
was as sound as it was brilliant.   He had the instinct
of the journalist, and was never at a loss for an
appropriate heading.

Matthew Arnold's appearance was both impressive
and agreeable.   He was tall, of commanding presence,
with black hair, which never became grey, and blue
eyes.   He was shortsighted, and his eye-glass gave him
a false air of superciliousness, accentuated by the clever
caricaturist of *Vanity Fair*.   In reality he was the most
genial and amiable of men.   But he had a good deal of
manner, which those who did not know him mistook for
assumption.   It was nothing of the kind, but a mixture
of old-fashioned courtesy and comic exaggeration.   Mr.
Arnold was always willing to tell a story, or to join
in a laugh, against himself.   Roughness or rudeness he
could not bear.   He was essentially a polished man of
the world.   He never gave himself airs, or seemed
conscious of any superiority to those about him.   Con-
siderate politeness to young and old, rich and poor,
obscure and eminent, was the practice of his life.   His
standard was the standard of a Christian gentleman, his
models in that respect were such men as Newman and
Church.   He enjoyed not only, with the exception of
his hereditary complaint, good health and good spirits,
but one of those happy temperaments which diffuse and
radiate satisfaction.   No one could be cross or bored
when Matthew Arnold was in the room.   He was
always amusing, and always seemed to look at the

bright side of things.   Naturally sociable, and in a
modest way convivial, he took pleasure both in the
exercise and in the acceptance of hospitality.   He
knew good wine from bad, and was not ashamed to
admit the knowledge.   His talk was witty, pointed,
and often irresistibly droll.   Although public speaking
did not suit him, he had a very flexible voice, admirably fitted for the dramatic rendering of a story, or
for the purposes of satirical criticism.   He could be
very dogmatic in conversation, but never aggressive
or overbearing.   For a poet he was surprisingly practical, taking a lively interest in people's incomes, the
rent of their houses, the produce of their gardens, and
the size of their families.   He had none of Wordsworth's contempt for gossip, and his father's strenuous
earnestness had not descended to him.   " Habitually
indulging a strong propensity to mockery," as Macaulay
says of Halifax, he was never ill-natured, and never
willingly gave pain.   He would make fun of the people
he loved best, but he always did it good-humouredly.
His theoretical belief in the principle of authority had
little influence upon his practice.   Mr. Arthur Benson,
in his portly biography of his father, tells us how the
author of *Literature and Dogma*, on being confronted
with some paternal dictum, replied with his confiden-
tial smile, " Dear Dr. Arnold was not infallible."   Mr.
Arnold's smile was like a touch of nature, it made the
whole world kin.

It is not unnatural to compare or contrast Matthew
Arnold with his two great contemporaries, Tennyson
and Browning.   Tennyson was born thirteen years,
Browning eleven years, before him.   Browning survived him by a year, Tennyson by four years.   Tenny-

son stands almost alone in literature as a poet, and
nothing but a poet, throughout his long life. All his
scholarship, all his knowledge, all the speculative
power of his wonderful mind, went into poetry, and
into poetry alone. Browning, though he had no pro-
fession, was as constantly in the world as Tennyson
was constantly out of it. He lived two lives, the
imaginative and the actual, with equal zest. Matthew
Arnold was as sociable as Browning, and as genuine
a poet. But he had to work for his living, and either
the Education Department or the critical faculty almost
dried up the poetic vein. It was not that the quality
of his verse deteriorated, as the quality of Browning's
did, and as the quality of Tennyson's did not. What
little poetry he wrote at the end of his life was good,
and in the case of "Westminster Abbey," very good.
But he ceased as a poet to be productive. The energies
of his mind were drawn into politics, into theology,
into literary criticism. There was much in him of
his father's missionary zeal. He longed to make the
world better, though by other means and in other
directions than Dr. Arnold's. His spiritual father
was Wordsworth, from whose grave his own poetry
may be said to have sprung. Wordsworth lived to
be much older than Mr. Arnold, and, though his prose
is exquisite, there is not much of it. In him, too,
great poet as he was, the imagination dwindled and
decayed. After middle age he produced little that
lives. Tennyson remained to the end as magical, as
imaginative, as musical, as he had ever been. We
cannot estimate Matthew Arnold's greatness if we
separate his poetry from his criticism. His theological and political writings prove his versatility without

adding much to his permanent reputation. It is as the poet and critic, the man who practised what he preached, that he survives. He was an incarnate contradiction of the false epigram that the critics are those who have failed in literature and art.

The great fault of his prose, especially of his later prose, is repetition. He had, like Mr. Brooke in *Middlemarch*, a marked tendency to say what he had said before. His defect as a poet was the imperfection of his ear for rhythm. But, as Johnson said of Goldsmith, " enough of his failings; he was a very great man." Such poetry as *Mycerinus*, such prose as the Preface of the *Essays in Criticism*, are enough to make a man a classic, and to preserve his memory from decay.

N

INDEX

ENGLISH MEN OF LETTERS

EDITED BY

JOHN MORLEY

Cloth. 12mo. Price, 40 cents, each

ADDISON. By W. J. Courthope.

BACON. By R. W. Church.

BENTLEY. By Prof. Jebb.

BUNYAN. By J. A. Froude.

BURKE. By John Morley.

BURNS. By Principal Shairp.

BYRON. By Prof. Nichol.

CARLYLE. By Prof. Nichol.

CHAUCER. By Prof. A. W. Ward.

COLERIDGE. By H. D. Traill.

COWPER. By Goldwin Smith.

DEFOE. By W. Minto.

DE QUINCEY. By Prof. Masson.

DICKENS. By A. W. Ward.

DRYDEN. By G. Saintsbury.

FIELDING. By Austin Dobson.

GIBBON. By J. Cotter Morison.

GOLDSMITH. By William Black.

GRAY. By Edmund Gosse.

HUME. By T. H. Huxley.

JOHNSON. By Leslie Stephen.

KEATS. By Sidney Colvin.

LAMB. By Alfred Ainger.

LANDOR. By Sidney Colvin.

LOCKE. By Prof. Fowler.

MACAULAY.
By J. Cotter Morison.

MILTON. By Mark Pattison.

POPE. By Leslie Stephen.

SCOTT. By R. H. Hutton.

SHELLEY. By J. A. Symonds.

SHERIDAN. By Mrs. Oliphant.

SIR PHILIP SIDNEY.
By J. A. Symonds.

SOUTHEY. By Prof. Dowden.

SPENSER. By R. W. Church.

STERNE. By H. D. Traill.

SWIFT. By Leslie Stephen.

THACKERAY. By A. Trollope.

WORDSWORTH.
By F. W. H. Myers.

NEW VOLUMES

Cloth. 12mo. Price, 75 cents net

GEORGE ELIOT. By Leslie Stephen.

WILLIAM HAZLITT. By Augustine Birrell.

MATTHEW ARNOLD. By Herbert W. Paul.

JOHN RUSKIN. By Frederic Harrison.

ALFRED TENNYSON. By Alfred Lyall.

ENGLISH MEN OF LETTERS

EDITED BY

JOHN MORLEY

THREE BIOGRAPHIES IN EACH VOLUME

Cloth. 12mo. Price, $1.00, each

CHAUCER. By Adolphus William Ward. **SPENSER.** By R. W. Church. **DRYDEN.** By George Saintsbury.

MILTON. By Mark Pattison, B.D. **GOLDSMITH.** By William Black. **COWPER.** By Goldwin Smith.

BYRON. By John Nichol. **SHELLEY.** By John Addington Symonds. **KEATS.** By Sidney Colvin, M.A.

WORDSWORTH. By F. W. H. Myers. **SOUTHEY.** By Edward Dowden. **LANDOR.** By Sidney Colvin, M.A.

LAMB. By Alfred Ainger. **ADDISON.** By W. J. Courthope. **SWIFT.** By Leslie Stephen.

SCOTT. By Richard H. Hutton. **BURNS.** By Principal Shairp. **COLERIDGE.** By H. D. Traill.

HUME. By T. H. Huxley, F.R.S. **LOCKE.** By Thomas Fowler. **BURKE.** By John Morley.

FIELDING. By Austin Dobson. **THACKERAY.** By Anthony Trollope. **DICKENS.** By Adolphus William Ward.

GIBBON. By J. Cotter Morison. **CARLYLE.** By John Nichol. **MACAULAY.** By J. Cotter Morison.

SIDNEY. By J. A. Symonds. **DE QUINCEY.** By David Masson. **SHERIDAN.** By Mrs. Oliphant.

POPE. By Leslie Stephen. **JOHNSON.** By Leslie Stephen. **GRAY.** By Edmund Gosse.

BACON. By R. W. Church. **BUNYAN.** By J. A. Froude. **BENTLEY.** By R. C. Jebb.

PUBLISHED BY

THE MACMILLAN COMPANY

66 FIFTH AVENUE, NEW YORK